The Help Desk Handbook

The Help Desk Institute

guide to Help Desk operations

and problem management

Ron Muns

Help
Desk
Institute

Editor-in-chief

Patrick Bultema

Managing editor

James Etchison

Associate editor

Patrice Rhoades-Baum

Assistant editor

Lyneen Johnson

Contributing editors

Char LaBounty
David Dell

 **Help Desk Institute**

*Training, educational materials and a
networking forum for Help Desk professionals.*

Help Desk Institute
1755 Telstar Drive, Suite 101
Colorado Springs, CO 80920-1017
US and Canada 800-248-5667
Worldwide 719-531-5138

Table of contents

About Help Desk Institute

Help Desk Institute was formed to provide training, educational materials, and a networking forum for Help Desk professionals. Since its inception, tens of thousands of Help Desk professionals have participated, as members and attendees, in educational programs and industry conferences across the United States, Canada, Australia, and Europe.

Since the Institute's first round-table symposium, *The Guide to Help Desk/Problem Management*, Help Desk Institute has created a variety of programs and services designed to meet the changing needs of the technical and customer support professional. Many of these benefits (listed on the right) are free to Institute members as part of their annual membership package. Other benefits are available at generous member discounts.

More than 40 Help Desk Institute Local Chapters, locally formed and operated, are already thriving in the United States, Canada, Australia, and Europe. At regular Local Chapter meetings, support professionals exhange ideas, discuss common concerns and take advantage of special Institute services.

Help Desk Institute is your support center. We keep you up to date with the latest training and information on tools and industry trends. Some of the world's largest organizations know that a Help Desk Institute membership is a cost-effective way to keep its Help Desk and customer support people informed and productive.

Help Desk Institute's Programs and Services

- The annual International Help Desk Conference

- Seminars, symposiums, and conferences offered year-round throughout the U.S., Canada, Europe, and Australia

- In-house seminars and consulting services

- Help Desk U© – a series of self-directed learning courses for Help Desk professionals

- Critical industry research

- *Liferaft* ®, the Institute's bimonthly newsletter that provides ideas and case studies to help members improve the operation of their Help Desk or support center

- *The Help Desk Handbook*

- Member discounts on all seminars, conferences, and publications

- *The Help Desk Buyer's Guide*

- Cross-referenced Directory of Members

- An opportunity to serve on the HDI Advisory Board or as a Local Chapter officer

- HDI Members have six months free access the Help Desk Institute on-line forums on ZiffNet.

- The Help Desk Institute Bookstore

- Industry surveys on current Help Desk structure, operation, and salary trends

- Vendor exhibit showcases

Introduction

To increase the productivity of people using information technology in a company, you need to provide an efficient and effective means to answer their questions and solve their problems. The mission of a Help Desk is just that easy ... and that hard. Easy because the need is clear. After all, every person who uses a computer has questions or problems at one time or another. These questions and problems are often frustrating for the person to solve. Often, these problems result in significant losses in productivity. It's no surprise, then, that recent studies have shown the cost of supporting a computer workstation each year is two to three times the cost of buying the workstation.

Although the mission is clear, how you accomplish the mission quickly becomes a complicated question. What telecommunications technologies should you use ... ACD, auto attendant, IVRU, audio text, and call management systems? What problem tracking software should you use? How will you capture the expertise you need at a Help Desk, so you can answer your customers' questions and solve their problems? How should you organize and manage your support center? What type of person should you hire, and what training should you provide for that agent? The list goes on and on. In fact, for many new and even experienced customer support managers, the amount of information you need to know, the skills you need to have, and the trends you need to track are simply overwhelming.

That's why this book is so important to the Help Desk and Customer Support industry. In one volume, it presents the most important information you need to know. It helps you think through the decisions you need to make. And it provides you with the perspective and practical advice you need to make the right decisions ... the first time.

This book is also important, because of the expert who stands behind it, Ron Muns. Ron is recognized as *the* international leader of the Help Desk industry. Founder of Help Desk Institute, Ron has lead Executive Roundtables for Help Desk professionals, and provided training and consulting for thousands of support organizations around the world. So you can count on the breadth of knowledge and practical experience on these pages.

Both Ron and the Help Desk Institute acknowledge and thank the many ideas and contributions of Help Desk Institute members that have shaped our ideas and thinking about our industry. And we especially thank people who have submitted sample documents, reports, and systems screens to include in this book ... Aspect Telecommunications, Avco Financial Services, Bendata Management Systems, IDS Financial Services, Remedy Corporation, Taco Bell Corporation, and Wyeth-Ayerst Labs.

Our commitment is to make *The Help Desk Handbook* the definitive handbook for the Help Desk and Customer Support industry. To that end, we welcome your questions, comments, or suggestions on how we can make this book even better in future editions. That's why we've included a postage-paid comment form in the back of the book. So thank you in advance for you comments. And thank you for reading *The Help Desk Handbook*.

Patrick Bultema
Director, Product Development
Help Desk Institute
November 1993

chapter 1

Purposes and objectives of the Help Desk

How did the Help Desk develop, and how will it change to meet the demands and goals of the future? In this chapter, we'll present an overview of Help Desks of the past, present, and future. We'll also review the activities of the typical Help Desk and focus on the purposes and objectives of the Help Desk. Finally, we'll discuss current trends that will help shape the Help Desk of tomorrow.

Origins of the Help Desk

Help Desks have existed in many forms since the early days of computers. For our purposes, the term *Help Desk* means the part of the data processing effort that answers questions or coordinates the resolution of problems that customers encounter while using

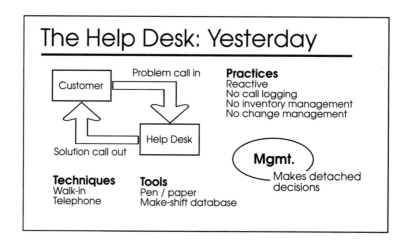

Figure 1-1   The Help Desk of the past

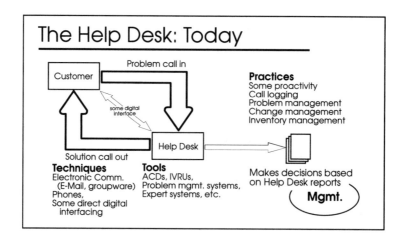

Figure 1-2   A typical Help Desk of today

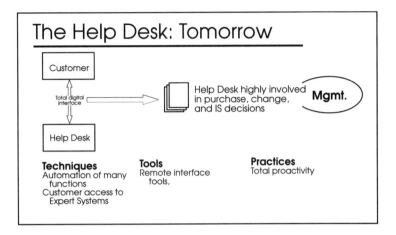

The Help Desk: Tomorrow

Customer

Total digital interface

Help Desk

Help Desk highly involved in purchase, change, and IS decisions

Mgmt.

Techniques
Automation of many functions
Customer access to Expert Systems

Tools
Remote interface tools,

Practices
Total proactivity

Figure 1-3   A possible Help Desk of the future

computer hardware and software. Customers of the Help Desk may be external clients of the company or internal customers – employees using the company's own applications and systems.

In many organizations, the methods of providing help to customers evolved over the years as companies applied data processing to more and more functions. In some cases, customers had one number to call for hardware problems, another for software questions on the mainframe, another for PC questions, and possibly even a different number for teleprocessing or network problems.

In recent years, companies have followed a trend of consolidating the various customer support areas into one Help Desk function. This trend provides a central contact point for customers to call to resolve problems. The central Help Desk also helps create an audit trail, documentation of problem resolutions, and a central repository of problem information for analysis purposes.

The Information Center, the predecessor of the Help Desk, became popular in the early 1980s for most large U.S. companies. In many of these companies, the Information Center has now become part of the Help Desk or the point at which agents handle initial calls.

In addition, vendors have encouraged organizations to centralize problem management and reporting. This encouragement has come in the form of cost-saving discounts. For example, IBM's customer service agreement reduces maintenance fees to customers willing to meet certain criteria.

Figures 1-1 through 1-3 graphically represent Help Desk practices, techniques, and tools of the past, present, and – possibly – the future.

Help Desk activities

Today, Help Desk and problem management activities focus on answering customers' questions when possible and appropriate. The Help Desk resolves and coordinates the resolution of customer problems and acts as the liaison between the data center technical staff and the customer community. These basic functions help define the purposes and objectives of the Help Desk.

From a customer's point of view, the Help Desk represents a single source of help. This is true even if the resources required to address the customer's needs involve several persons or groups. Centralizing customer support helps ensure customer satisfaction because it shelters the customer from the frustration of personally following a problem as it passes to different data processing service personnel.

When the customer community includes key customers or departments that require priority responses, the Help Desk ensures this level of service by commanding the appropriate resources. For the typical customer call, the Help Desk provides the first level of problem resolution – often the sole source of help required. On average, the Help Desk directly resolves 71% of customer problems (from Help Desk Institute's 1993 *Help Desk Practices Survey.*)

The Help Desk benefits the customer community in many ways beyond providing a single source of help. These benefits are not always immediately apparent to individual customers. For example, by logging and tracking calls from all customers, the Help Desk is uniquely positioned to identify customers' training and education needs to further their knowledge and productivity. The Help Desk can gather and communicate problem-tracking information to help the organization plan to add hardware, software, and procedures that better meet the customers' needs.

Besides aiding the customer community, the Help Desk serves as a valuable resource for the information processing technical staff. By documenting, assessing, and routing problem calls, the Help Desk reduces the requirement for personal contacts with customers by the technical staff, allowing the technical staff to be more productive.

Help Desk reporting of problem status and history can foster an overall improvement in quality of service. Help Desks can provide key information to management on problem trends that would be otherwise unavailable, making earlier identification of problems possible and providing better data for problem resolution analysis. In addition, by analyzing and addressing the root causes of problems, the Help Desk can help eliminate many of these problems as well as the calls they cause.

The unique intermediary position the Help Desk holds also opens new possibilities for improving information processing services throughout an organization. The Help Desk can identify customer requirements and service expectations; evaluate the effectiveness of

---

Help Desk mission statement

Maximize operational efficiency in the organization by providing timely resolution to operations questions and effectively manage these problems to continuously improve the quality of the Help Desk service, the usability of the system, and the effectiveness of training.

Figure 1-4   **Example of a mission statement from a typical Help Desk**

products, vendors, and staff; and compile and report these findings to the organization's management team.

In defining the purposes and objectives of your Help Desk – and establishing the staff and procedures to meet those purposes and objectives – your organization can achieve a quality information processing service that meets the current and future needs of your customer community.

Help Desk objectives

Figure 1-4 presents an example of a mission statement from a typical Help Desk. The following points discuss the purposes and objectives of the Help Desk in greater detail.

Serve the customer community   The Help Desk provides a single contact point representing Information Services (IS) for the customer community.

Resolve problems   Agents help their customers resolve problems quickly, log all problem calls, and maintain total accountability for the service event until problems are completely resolved. You also monitor problems assigned to support personnel to ensure adequate and timely resolution, communicate the resolution to customers, and close out problems that are satisfactorily resolved.

Agents need to resolve as many problem calls at the Help Desk as possible to reduce the number of calls assigned to additional support personnel and maximize the IS group's productivity. You also improve the productivity of other technical personnel by functioning as the initial contact point for all problems.

Improve the productivity of the customer community   The Help Desk tracks and manages difficult problems and provides the mechanism to handle critical problems and escalate their priority whenever necessary. The Help Desk also identifies recurring problems, reports trends to management, and recommends system fixes or additional customer training and education as appropriate. This organization also provides real-time notification to customers regarding serious problems, expected time-to-resolution, and actual problem resolution.

Change management   The Help Desk also coordinates changes in software and hardware to ensure a smooth transition for customers and operations. Agents communicate information to customers regarding known problems, upcoming changes, educational opportunities, and methods of improving productivity.

Measure the Help Desk's activities   The Help Desk develops standard management reports and special focus reports to draw management's attention to correctable problems and important trends. You can use problem history to improve the availability and reliability of the systems that Information Services provides. You can also collect data to measure the performance and service levels of vendors and internal service partners.

Trends

Organizational purposes and objectives evolve over time, depending on demands and available technology. Nine current trends affecting the purposes, objectives, and operational procedures of the Help Desk follow.

Realizing the Help Desk's value   Companies are increasingly recognizing the Help Desk's value to the organization's overall business – possibly resulting in increased visibility and broader scope of responsibility for the Help Desk.

Emphasizing customer service   Help Desks are placing an expanded emphasis on the importance of high-quality customer service. As a result, Help Desks and customers are working together to prioritize service problems.

Running "leaner and meaner"   The nationwide trend toward downsizing in organizations can impact the Help Desk by expecting it to run with fewer staff members and expecting the Help Desk to take more pressure off other support organizations by resolving more problems at the first level. Over time, Help Desk personnel may evolve from traditional phone support to engineers maintaining technology.

Centralization of Help Desks   Companies are following the trend of consolidating smaller Help Desks into larger, centralized units. Generally, this allows staff reductions while facilitating the "one place to call" concept so important to customer convenience.

Using technology   Help Desks are choosing and implementing tools such as enhanced expert system (artificial intelligence) tools to assist the Help Desk in problem resolution; on-line hypertext-type systems to store, update, and retrieve procedural information; telephone system tie-ins to problem management such as voice mail, fax, and voice response units; and CD technology for reference information

Using technology to meet objectives   Help Desks are using more technology to meet their objectives. Without these tools, Help Desks cannot meet the goal of increasing service and responsibilities while holding down staff growth.

Coordinating change   Help Desks are playing a larger role in coordinating change. Its role as a dispassionate client advocate uniquely positions the Help Desk to influence other IS units' priorities. The results would be improved system stability and customers' improved perceptions of the IS department.

Sharing LAN support issues   Help Desks are increasingly sharing overall problems represented by LAN support issues. The tools, processes, and organizational structures required to support LANs and client/server technology are in their early evolutionary stages. In many ways, support for these technologies today roughly parallels support for mainframe computers in the early 1970s.

Developing customer applications   Help Desks will continue to help develop future customer applications with built-in help systems.

chapter **2**

Organizing
the Help Desk

If you are charged with developing a new Help Desk facility or managing a group of existing Help Desks, you face a variety of choices concerning the best way to design your organization.

This chapter presents key issues to consider when organizing your Help Desk. We'll discuss management and customer requirements, creating centralized or decentralized Help Desk teams, and establishing support structures within the Help Desk. We'll also discuss the ways your customers contact you and other Help Desk agents – whether by telephone, message center, or E-mail. Finally, we'll discuss communication needs within the Help Desk and using tools – such as on-line problem management systems – and procedures – such as shift turnover meetings – to meet these needs.

Management and customer requirements

Your organization exists to serve your customer community, so your primary goal will always be to design your organization to meet these requirements. Some requirements to consider include your hours of operation, urgency of support, and the diversity of your customer community.

Hours of operation   The longer your hours of service, the more expensive it is to staff your Help Desk. If you're expected to be available seven days a week, 24 hours a day, a significant part of your overhead may be staffing one or two agents to take calls during low-volume hours on nights and weekends. Because of this overhead, it is sometimes more effective to handle a wide variety of calls with a single Help Desk to reduce the per-call cost of your operation.

Urgency of support   If your Help Desk is a key escalation point for major systems problems, you usually need to keep more staff available than would be required under normal non-crisis conditions. Some operations handle this by having more people available on the phones, while others opt to create a small, separate unit to handle major problems or recurring problems that result in major customer dissatisfaction. This unit can handle longer-term project work when operations are running smoothly.

Diversity of customer community   If your Help Desk serves a relatively homogenous customer community, consider combining multiple functions into a larger group, since your staff's training needs are simplified. Conversely, a wide variety of customers with different problems and expectations demand customer-specific training and usually makes some group separation more effective.

Centralized Help Desks

Advantages

1. Customers have fewer questions about who to call

2. Generally lower in staffing require-ments and more stability of service levels, since a larger staff pool can absorb peaks

3. More flexible staffing for vacations and sick days

Figure 2-1   **The advantages of centralized Help Desks**

Centralized Help Desks

Disadvantages

1. More difficult to keep staff trained in all the different applications and support offerings

2. Can result in fewer problems resolved at the first level due to a trade-off of depth of knowledge for breadth of coverage

3. More need for specialists to assist the front-line staff

Figure 2-2   **The disadvantages of centralized Help Desks**

Decentralized Help Desks

Advantages

1. Able to customize support for a specific customer community and able to maintain a deeper agent knowledge due to narrower focus

2. Easier to train for narrower knowledge base and can hire for specific knowledge areas

Figure 2-3   **The advantages of decentralized Help Desks**

Decentralized Help Desks

Disadvantages

1. Service levels such as hold time are more sensitive to temporary staff shortages or high call volumes

2. Customers must know which group to call or which area to select from a voice menu

Figure 2-4   **The disadvantages of decentralized Help Desks**

Centralized or decentralized Help Desk teams

Several factors contribute to your decision of whether to consolidate multiple smaller Help Desks into a larger, centralized entity or decentralize a large Help Desk by creating several satellite, decentralized units. Figures 2-1 through 2-4 summarize the advantages and disadvantages associated with each approach. Remember, these generalizations may not apply to your organization.

1. Tracking problem trends and recurring problems

2. Conducting and reporting on customer surveys

3. Producing management reports reflecting Help Desk and vendor service levels

4. Developing and maintaining new procedures for Help Desk staff

5. Developing Help Desk training programs

6. Supporting change management activities

7. Acting as application specialists for particularly complex applications or procedures

8. Providing end-to-end problem management for critical or difficult-to-resolve problems

Figure 2-5   **Eight tasks for functional units within the Help Desk**

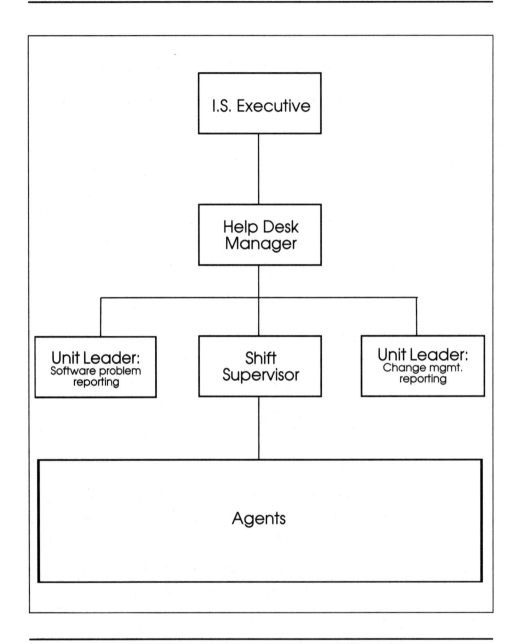

Figure 2-6   **Organization chart of a typical Help Desk organization**

Support structures within the Help Desk

For larger Help Desks, you may want to separate some of your staff into functional units that are not directly responsible for handling calls. Figure 2-5 presents possible tasks such functional units may work on. And Figure 2-6 shows how these units fit into the Help Desk's organization.

The principle idea behind this support structure is to ensure staff members can accomplish key activities despite the day-to-day crises that often overwhelm the call-handling staff. Remember, you can use a flexible organizational structure to accomplish these tasks – you can staff these areas permanently or on a rotating basis.

Customer interface

You can provide customers with access to your Help Desk resources in a variety of ways. The most commonly used approaches are direct Help Desk staff access, staffed message centers, and walk-up Help Desks.

Direct Help Desk staff access

Direct Help Desk staff access is the most common form of customer interface. In this approach, a Help Desk agent directly answers the customer's call, usually after the customer makes a selection on a voice menu. The staff member then provides immediate assistance or call routing. This method provides customers with immediate feedback and lets them know the Help Desk is promptly addressing their problem. It also provides Help Desk agents the opportunity to ask questions to ensure they record all necessary information during the first call; this keeps customers from having to restate the problem during future calls.

The number of calls the Help Desk can receive is limited by the number of available Help Desk agents and their ability to handle each call in a timely fashion. When there are more calls than available agents, customers usually hear a recorded message and must wait for an agent. Some voice mail features give customers the option of leaving a message as an alternative to waiting in queue.

Message center

A message center is similar to voice mail and direct access; the customer leaves a message regarding the problem and the appropriate Help Desk staff member returns the call. The customer may have to repeat the problem to the agent or other person if the call is routed further after the initial return call.

Some firms report that if customers do not receive immediate personal attention, they sometimes resolve a problem on their own by using manuals or other available resources such as fellow customers. This method may reduce calls to the Help Desk by 50%. However, this may not be the desired result if your Help Desk strives to ensure a high level of personal service. This situation can also encourage informal support structures to develop; these structures cost the organization in lost productivity and are contrary to the main purpose for having a Help Desk.

The Gartner Group estimates that for every $1 companies spend on formal support functions, they spend $3 on informal support (co-workers, friends, and supervisors). Thus, the Help Desk's contribution to productivity has a major impact on the organization's bottom line.

A message center can also frustrate customers and Help Desk agents if customers are not available to take returned calls and games of telephone tag ensue.

1. On-line problem management systems

2. Daily morning meetings

3. Shift turnover meetings

4. Departmental meetings

5. Bulletin boards and posting areas

6. Electronic mail

7. Management reports

8. On-line or paper-based procedures

Figure 2-7   **Methods for communicating within the Help Desk**

Walk-up Help Desks

Some firms provide walk-up Help Desks for their customers. With this method, the Help Desk is located in a common, non-restricted area and available Help Desk personnel service the customers. Customers who take advantage of the walk-up Help Desk typically wish to drop off or discuss hard copy examples of their problems. Such problems often include report formats and screen prints of error codes.

Communication within the Help Desk

You have several options for intercommunication within your Help Desk, depending on the size and type of your organization. Figure 2-7 presents some common methods. Some of these options include on-line problem management systems; daily morning meetings, shift turnover meetings, and departmental meetings; bulletin boards and posting areas; E-mail; management reports; and on-line or paper-based procedures.

Whichever communication approaches your organization uses, getting information to all Help Desk staff members can be a challenge, particularly if you run a seven-day, 24-hour operation. For example, midnight shift staff members usually can't attend staff meetings, and can be easily left out. For these agents, it's particularly important to record staff information either in written form or by group voice mail. It's also a good idea for managers to periodically visit midnight shifts to make sure the staff has access to a manager for questions and discussions.

chapter **3**

Physical Help Desk arrangements

The physical layout of your Help Desk can significantly impact the productivity of the staff. Don't take the physical layout for granted; it can influence agents' stress levels and their ability to diagnose and solve problems.

The ideal location of the Help Desk depends on the nature of the problems handled, the location of the customer community, and the location of the primary, level-two and level-three support personnel. Other factors influencing the location include the need for security, the desire for providing walk-up access for help (or tours) and the location of the Help Desk manager.

In this chapter, we'll review how your work environment impacts your productivity as well as how specialized tools – such as special telephone equipment,

Figure 3-1 **Strategic placement of short and tall cubicle dividers, shown here, will optimize inter-agent communication while still providing privacy. (Photo courtesy of Corporate Software, Canton, MA.)**

multiscreen monitors, and problem management software – help you better perform your job.

Work environment

A number of issues impact the working environment. For instance, though most people enjoy working in a private office, this does not appear to be effective for Help Desk work. Agents say they need contact with others during problem resolution. It's common for several Help Desk personnel to be involved in short discussions to resolve problems or coordinate actions during a crisis. Be sure to consider this need for interaction in your space layout planning.

Figure 3-2   Headsets free agents' hands and reduce neck strain. (Photo courtesy of Aspect Telecommunications.)

Figure 3-1 illustrates a way to resolve the need for agents' privacy by providing short walls between Help Desk workstations. Walls 42 to 45 inches high provide privacy when the staff person is seated and allow for easy conversations when individuals need to discuss solutions.

If your organization offers a walk-up Help Desk or frequent tours, you'll need to consider customer access. Route the flow of visitors to minimize interference with the work of the staff.

1. Special-purpose telephone equipment

2. Personal computers, multiscreen monitors, and multitasking software

3. Help Desk diagnostic, tracking, and problem management software

4. On-line or paper-based procedures documentation

5. Network maps

6. Electronic status displays or white boards

7. Fax machine

8. Phone directories on-line or printed and bound

9. Monitor software that allows Help Desk agents to view the customers' terminals or PC interactions from the Help Desk

Figure 3-3   Specialized tools for the Help Desk

Reducing noise levels in the area helps personnel remain calm while talking with customers, working on problems, and dealing with others. To decrease the noise at your Help Desk, consider carpeting the floors and walks, providing plants to absorb sounds, using noise dampening furniture and walls, and introducing white noise to soothe or eliminate the impact of background conversations.

Lighting in the Help Desk work area should produce a minimum amount of glare on the computer terminals. Such lighting could come from indirect light provided by incandescent bulbs rather than fluorescent lights. You can accomplish this by using a track lighting system above each work station.

When planning the layout of agents' workstations, be sure to provide adequate space for monitors, reference materials, phones, modems, and work surfaces. And when purchasing furniture, remember that comfortable, ergonomic chairs are among the best investments to increase staff productivity and improve employees' attitudes. A chair that provides adequate back support – as well as mobility within the individuals' working space – increases productivity and reduces the possibility of back injury.

Telephone headsets also increase productivity and are rapidly becoming the standard method for receiving calls. Figure 3-2 shows how headsets free the agents' hands and reduce neck strain.

In addition, as incidents of repetitive stress injuries such as carpal tunnel syndrome continue to increase, it's important to consider special keyboard platforms and other ergonomic desk arrangements to minimize the risk of injury.

Specialized tools

Equipment at the Help Desk consists of the tools the staff members need to perform their jobs. Figure 3-3 presents a brief list of some of these tools. The equipment your Help Desk requires depends on the technology you support and the nature of problem calls you receive. Specialized tools might include special-purpose telephone equipment, multiscreen monitors, Help Desk diagnostic and problem management software, electronic status displays, and monitor software that allows you to view the customer's terminal or PC interaction from the Help Desk.

chapter **4**

Staffing the Help Desk

To create an effective Help Desk, you need to first determine your staff needs, then work to build a team of agents who can provide the best service to your customers and help your organization meet its goals.

In this chapter, we'll discuss how to determine staff needs, and we'll present skills and personality traits beneficial to Help Desk agents. We'll discuss the issue of hiring generalists or specialists. And we'll present ideas on training Help Desk agents and establishing job descriptions. Next, the section on team building and stress management techniques will help keep you and your Help Desk running in top condition.

1. Incoming calls

2. Outbound calls/notification

3. Obtaining data

4. Recording incidents

5. Diagnosing problems

6. Analyzing problems

7. Assigning problems

8. Resolving problems

9. Closing problems

Figure 4-1   **Key functions required of most Help Desks**

How to determine staff needs

To determine staff needs, you must define the main functions of your Help Desk. Figure 4-1 presents a list of some of these functions. Key functions at your Help Desk probably include answering incoming calls, recording incidents, and diagnosing, resolving, and closing problems.

Help Desk skills

Hiring individuals with the appropriate skills and personal characteristics is vital to the success of any Help Desk. The technical skills required of Help Desk personnel depends on the level of service your Help Desk provides and the complexity of the calls you

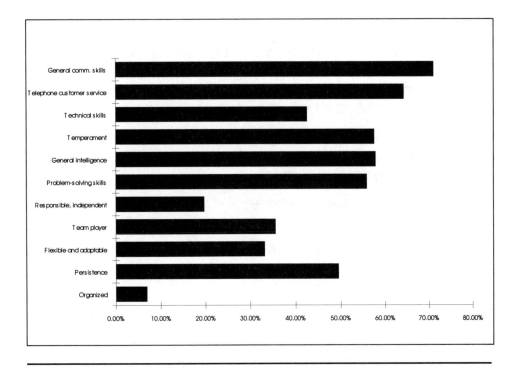

Figure 4-2 The 11 most desirable skills found in Help Desk agents, ranked by participants of Help Desk Institute's 1993 Help Desk Practices Survey

receive. Most organizations require Help Desk personnel to have general computer knowledge. Other necessary skills such as PC or network knowledge vary greatly among organizations.

The required technical skills can be quantified analyzing call history; the number of calls for different types of problems will reveal the skills your Help Desk personnel need.

Figure 4-2 shows how participants in Help Desk Institute's 1993 Help Desk Practices Survey ranked the various skills they look for in Help Desk agents.

The level of automation your Help Desk uses to record and analyze calls also influences needed skills. In

1. Evaluate statistics on the number of calls handled by time of day, day of week, agent, time on phone and repsonse time, time available to take calls, and rolled and abandoned calls.

2. Review the systems and procedures the Help Desk uses including problem, configuration, and change management.

3. Quantify your service-level commitment to your customers.

4. Determine customer satisfaction with your Help Desk's service through frequent customer surveys.

Figure 4-3   Four items to consider when determining the optimum size of your Help Desk staff

addition, the number of customers and types of systems the Help Desk supports governs your staffing decisions. You also need to consider the expertise of your customers, whether they are essentially self-sufficient or technically demanding. Published job descriptions allow you to make recruiting decisions based upon the required skills.

Call tracking and analysis can also help define skill requirements and the number of personnel needed to staff the Help Desk. Analyze the number of calls by totals and by employee.

Another mechanism for understanding Help Desk responsiveness and productivity is using automatic call distribution (ACD) statistics – information such as the number of calls handled by time of day, day of week, agent, time on phone and time to answer, time available to take calls, and rolled and abandoned calls. Most automated call distribution reporting systems can obtain this information. Analyzing additional statistics such as problem call volumes for each piece of hardware and software can also help you determine your staffing needs.

Figure 4-3 presents items to consider when establishing the staff size of a service-effective Help Desk. To set a service-effective staff size, evaluate the Help Desk's statistics, review the problem and change management systems, quantify your service-level commitment to your customers, and conduct frequent surveys to determine customer satisfaction.

When you evaluate your staffing requirements, compare call trends by type and actual performance to your service level commitments and staff levels. When possible, project historical and current trends to notify your management when staff changes might be needed to maintain and improve the level of your service.

General skills and personality traits

Although the experience required of staff members is typically learned on the job, some general skills and personality traits are desirable in Help Desk personnel. Some of these traits include good communication skills, team player attitudes, a tolerance to stress, and a strong technical background.

These skills and traits provide a solid starting point for establishing and maintaining a well-staffed and sufficiently experienced Help Desk team. Your Help Desk may drive additional, important staffing issues. By analyzing your call history, service level commitments, and resulting job requirements, you can understand your staffing requirements and more efficiently meet the needs of your customer community.

Specialists versus generalists

One of the main questions that arises when developing job descriptions for the Help Desk is when to hire specialists versus generalists. To properly address this, you need to understand each term.

A specialist has in-depth skills in one or more areas, such as programming, telecommunications, or specific applications. A generalist, in most cases, has overall computer, analytical and personal communications skills but may lack specialized experience.

Staffing the Help Desk with generalists can result in a more customer-oriented service. Since customers do not have to locate the specialist, the agent who answers the call can serve them. However, if the Help Desk has a large volume of complex calls from technical customers, then generalists may provide an inadequate level of support. In addition, the way your Help Desk is organized – centralized or decentralized – will influence your decision. For normal situations, a workable compromise might be to mostly staff generalists and a limited number of specialists.

Job descriptions

Job descriptions vary among organizations, depending on the corporate structure and how you have established the Help Desk within that structure. Several factors influence determining job descriptions including levels of experience, aptitudes, responsibilities, organizational structure, normal working hours, and method of evaluation.

Help Desk call dispatcher

Summary description

Responsible for inputting all undocumented communication (i.e, fax, written, recorded, and terminal messages) into the automated tracking data base

Essential job functions

Perform basic receptionist duties

Operate Help Desk terminal including distributing phone calls, faxes, and terminal messages to the proper party for resolution

Enter telephone and terminal messages into automated tracking data base

Follow-up unanswered messages and advising appropriate headquarters and field personnel

Light typing

Non-essential job functions

Order department supplies

File status reports and/or correspondence

Photocopying

Distribute documentation

Send faxes

Qualifications and experience

Type 40 words per minute

PC proficiency and familiarity with various software packages

General receptionist experience

Good verbal and written communication skills

High school diploma

Figure 4-4   Sample job description for a Help Desk call dispatcher

Help Desk agent

Summary Description

Help customers who are having operation problems and system malfunctions.

Advise on and performs various transactions

Essential job functions

Receive customer problem reports and answer same under the guidance of a Help Desk agent II

Answer questions regarding system procedures, on-line transactions, system status, and downtime

Relay messages sent to or received from customers in a timely manner

Stay informed of all changes to the operating systems that effect customers

Relay requests for assistance that are outside the scope of the Help Desk to the appropriate group

Maintain records of corresponence received and responded to

Non-essential job functions

File reports/correspondence

Photocopying

Send faxes

May perform duties of call dispatcher

Qualifications and experience

Type 40 words per minute

Prior intercompany experience helpful

Good verbal and written communication skills

Some knowledge of LANs helpful

Good technical/mechanical aptitude

Good organizational skills

PC proficiency and familiarity with various software packages

High School diploma

Figure 4-5   Sample job description for a Help Desk agent

Senior Help Desk agent

Summary description

The resident expert on existing and new operating systems under development. Provides guidance and training on operating systems to all Help Desk Agents, while solving branch operating problems.Helps branches with policies and procedures relating to company operations and errors caused by system malfunctions.

Essential job functions

Answer questions regarding system procedures, on-line transactions, system status, and downtime procedures

Analyze operating problems and quickly arrive at workable solutions

Answer questions regarding installations, setups, error messages, and status

Relaying requests for assistance that are outside the scope of the Help Desk to the appropriate group

Prepare database correction requests

Stay informed of all policies and procedures that effect customers

May perform functions of immediate supervisor

Non-essential job functions

Send terminal messages for operational services and other departments

Send faxes

Prior company experience requried

BA or BS degree preferred

Qualifications and experience

Throrough knowledge of company operations

Thorough knowledge of company software and Help Desk software

Good analytical skills

Good verbal and written communication skills

Good technical and mechanical aptitude

PC and LAN skills

Prior company experience required

BA or BS preferred

Figure 4-6   Sample job description for a senior Help Desk agent

Help Desk supervisor

Summary description

Supervise Help Desk personnel in solving operating problems with systems related malfunctions with all company operations and automated systems. Act as a liaison with management in the development and maintenance of systems and procedures.

Essential job functions

Supervise Help Desk staff

Assist, guide, and train subordinate personnel in their assigned functions

Assist in the preparation of user requirements for changes in the existing systems or development of new systems

Analyze changes to existing procedures for user operating manuals

Maintain liaison with all divisions and departments and field operations to keep abreast of policy and procedural changes

Assign work and ensure service level agreements are met

Assist in selection of staff and formal reviews

Non-essential job functions

Maintain liaison with outside vendors

Review test results to ensure systems meet requirements

May perform tasks of immediate supervisor

Qualifications and experience

Thorough knowledge of all phases of the company's operations

Good organizational and supervisory skills

Working knowledge of accounting, math, and law

Ability to communicate and work with senior management and staff

Self-motivated

Goal-oriented

BA or BS degree

Figure 4-7   Sample job description for a Help Desk supervisor

Help Desk manager

Summary description

> Direct the Help Desk function and support company operations

> Act as a liaison in the development and maintenance of systems and procedures

> Serve as liaison to outside vendors of processing services

> Develop or help prepare user requirements for new systems

Essential job functions

> Direct system and operations support relative to the maintenance and enhancement of all operating systems

> Review user requirements for changes to existing systems or development of new systems. Develop or help prepare user requirements

> Review changes to existing procedures for user operating manuals

> Maintain liaison with all divisions to keep abreast of policy and procedure changes

> Assign work and ensure service level agreements are met

> Represent the department on task forces and cross-functional teams

> Oversee selection of staff

> Supervise subordinates and perform formal reviews

Non-essential job functions

> Review test results to ensure that systems meet requirements

> Assist, guide, and train subordinate persnonnel in their assigned functions

Qualifications and experience

> Thorough knowledge of the company's operations

> Supervision experience helpful

> Overall knowledge of laws under which we operate

> Working knowledge of all departments, accounting, math, law, communications, and computer systems required

> Excellent communications skills

> Self-motivated and goal oriented

> Able to communicate and work with senior management and staff

> BA or BS required, Master's preferred

Figure 4-8   Sample job description for a Help Desk Manager

Figures 4-4 through 4-8 present sample Help Desk job descriptions.

Level of Experience   Factors that determine the levels of experience required for Help Desk staff include categories and complexities of problems, service level desired, size of the department, and size of the organization.

Aptitudes   The same factors that apply to experience also influence needed aptitudes. Most Help Desks require agents to conduct some training and have knowledge of computer functions and capabilities. Good communication skills are also important. The aptitude levels of analysis and problem-solving skills depend on the service level desired.

Responsibilities   The level of responsibilities and task assignments depend on the desired service level for the department and the individual job assignments. Clearly state in the job description the amount of problem diagnosis and analysis expected. Clarify responsibilities for problem solving, assigning, escalation, management reporting, and matters such as crisis management. At times, Help Desk personnel may have significant responsibilities to pull together resources to resolve problems. Many larger Help Desks may have "team lead" roles defined for individuals who are not managers. This role has special responsibilities and requires special skills and experience.

Organizational structure   Job descriptions should clearly define multiple levels of responsibility and authority. You can clearly show this structure on an organization chart. The placement of the Help Desk in the Information Services organization can also impact management's expectations of the service. Consider these expectations in staffing requirements. For example, if the Help Desk is part of the Network Support organization, then an agent's strong networking background

1. Classroom offsite
2. Classroom onsite
3. Self-directed learning products
4. Computer-based training
5. Video training
6. Hands-on mentoring

Figure 4-9   Training formats

would be a major asset, both for effectiveness on the Help Desk and for the agent's career development.

Normal working hours   The job description should explain position requirements for starting time, breaks, meals, quitting time, shift rotation, overtime, personal time, flexible working hours, and vacations. Typically, Help Desks are strict on punctuality; be sure to explain this to prospective employees.

Method of evaluation   Job descriptions should explain the procedure for reviewing the quality of employees' work. Include the policy for pay increases and their frequency and present the career path for this position.

Training

Training is a key component of the successful Help Desk. Unfortunately, it's typical for Help Desk staff to be trained on-the-job. This approach assumes agents can quickly absorb all the skills necessary to do the job well. Frequently, it results in inadequately trained people serving as the main point of contact between IS and the customer community.

1. Telephone skills

2. Customer relations

3. Stress management

4. Time management

5. Problem management systems and procedures

6. Listening, thinking, and writing skills

7. Typing skills

8. Problem-solving skills

Figure 4-10   **Eight general skills agents can develop through training**

Training Formats

A variety of effective training formats are available including classroom off-site, classroom on-site, computer-based training, video training, hands-on mentoring, and self-directed learning products such as Help Desk Institute's Help Desk U© products. Figure 4-9 presents these learning formats.

In many cases, the format choice is a secondary consideration, driven by the training methods available and that most closely match the topics you need covered. For commonly taught subjects, however, courses may be available in several formats that meet your training objectives. Classroom training is generally more expensive but also more effective, since the question-and-answer interaction with the instructor is stimulating and

1. Network management

2. Hardware troubleshooting

3. Applications training

4. Voice management

5. Software applications

6. Company-specific hardware, soft-ware, and device configurations

Figure 4-11   **Six technical areas agents can develop through training**

reinforces learning for most students. For large groups, bringing the course in-house can save considerable expense.

Except for hands-on training, it usually helps to get the trainee away from the Help Desk environment during the training periods. Day-to-day crises and distractions at the Help Desk will overwhelm the concentration of even the most dedicated student.

Types of training

General skills training   Figure 4-10 presents general areas Help Desk agents may want training to improve skills. To establish a training plan for yourself or your Help Desk, assess strengths and weaknesses in these areas. Your training program should emphasize important skills in the areas of greatest need. For example, agents who move to the Help Desk because of their technical skills may benefit from training in telephone skills or customer relations.

Technical skills training   Figure 4-11 lists some technical skills training Help Desk agents may need to pursue. Help Desk personnel need to acquire technical skills appropriate to the type of calls your Help Desk receives and the agreed-upon levels of service your Help Desk provides. Examples of training related to technical skills include network management, hardware trouble-shooting, applications training, voice management, specialized software workshops, and company-specific hardware, software, and device configurations.

The number of technical topics you or your staff needs is site specific. And the depth of technical training should match the level of service you wish to provide for the type of calls you generally receive. If your Help Desk's objective is to resolve 95% of problem calls, then your staff will need to obtain greater technical skills than if your objective is more modest.

Training pays off

Training is vitally important. When given a high priority, it pays off with multiple benefits to the IS department, the Help Desk staff, the customer commu-nity, and the corporation. Agents' performance and productivity increase with the level of training provided. And the cost of training is small when compared to its benefits. In addition, training costs are only a fraction of other personnel expenses such as salaries, benefits, and overhead. Training also pays off in enhanced career development opportunities for the staff and in improved employee morale.

Training at your Help Desk should be a continual process. As technology changes and new applications are developed, ongoing education can help you and your Help Desk meet your customers' needs.

1. Flexibility

2. Open-mindedness

3. People orientation

4. Professional attitude

5. Communication skills

6. Positive outlook

7. Creativity

8. Patience

Figure 4-12   **Eight characteristics that can aid team building**

Team building

Teamwork makes the Help Desk function well overall and helps provide a consistent positive image to the customer community. Individuals in a team work together as one; each supports and works to help others accomplish the Help Desk's goals and the organization's goals.

A team can consist of generalists and specialists who provide multiple benefits for the customer community and the overall organization. A key factor contributing to team building is the "chemistry" among the individuals.

Figure 4-12 presents a list of positive traits that can aid Help Desk agents in working together as a team. Staff members do not need to be identical in abilities, personalities, and training, but should have and foster certain team-building traits such as flexibility, communication skills, a positive outlook, and a professional attitude.

To develop a team that works together, the manager or supervisor must stand up for the Help Desk and be proud of the team's work. The Help Desk manager must market the Help Desk continually, both internally and externally. Support can be verbal, but should include financial and professional advancement rewards. For example, budgeting for adequate salaries, training, hardware, space, software, and other resources goes a long way toward improving team attitude. To foster the team attitude, it's also important for the manager to evaluate and reward staff based on team goals, not just individual heroics.

Another team builder with universal appeal is the weekly or twice-monthly staff meetings. Here, you can share information with staff members and listen to their concerns. Managers need to take time to hear ideas as well as complaints. Staff meetings help keep you informed and help coordinate upcoming events. Finally, establishing a pattern of helping each other on varying topics is educational and helps staff members work together as a team.

Stress management

Stress is a physiological response to the perception of a stimulus that threatens to take us outside our normal comfort zone. Stress causes our bodies to release adrenaline, raise our heartbeats, heighten our awareness, and increase muscle tension. A common perception is that stress is always bad. On the contrary, some stress is a necessary and healthy part of our lives. People even seek out stress by riding roller coasters, going to scary movies, or participating in other exciting – and stressful – activities.

Figure 4-13   **How we get trapped in stressful behavior**

However, an excessively high amount of stress continued over a long period of time is unhealthy. Figure 4-13 shows how you can get trapped in a stress cycle. The result is **distress**, which is not a healthy state for your body. From this point on, we'll use the term stress to indicate a high level of stress that threatens to become distress.

Symptoms of stress

Any change in our life or job situation – even a temporary or positive change – results in stress and may require adaptation. The amount of stress this situation produces is equal to the amount of your resistance to the change.

"Fight or flight," an instinctive response in stressful situations, is the choice between showing aggression or

1. Lethargy

2. Elevated blood pressure

3. Headaches and illness

4. Anger

5. Anxiety

6. Poor attitude

7. Depression

8. Alcoholism or drug use

9. On-the-job accidents

10. Absenteeism

11. Job turnover

12. Difficulty concentrating

Figure 4-14   Twelve symptoms of stress

fear. In a normal business situation you need to control and manage this instinctive response. The urge to take out frustrations on customers or fellow Help Desk workers can be damaging.

Figure 4-14 lists symptoms of excessive stress. Some of these symptoms include lethargy, headaches, anger, anxiety, difficulty concentrating, alcoholism or drug use, and on-the-job accidents.

Well managed organizations work to reduce stress, and you can measure many of these symptoms to determine if the level of stress at your Help Desk is increasing

1. Alarm
2. Resistance
3. Exhaustion

Figure 4-15 **These three stages of the general adaptation syndrome are frequently associated with stress.**

or decreasing. Your company probably gathers statistics for absenteeism, turnover, on-the-job injuries, and situations requiring disciplinary action. Your company may also conduct an attitude survey to determine overall satisfaction as well as stress on the job.

Stress is frequently accompanied by the general adaptation syndrome. Figure 4-15 illustrates this syndrome and the three physical stages of dealing with stress: alarm, resistance and exhaustion.

When in the physical stage of alarm, your body prepares for fight or flight. Also while under stress, your reaction may be to resist change; resistance is a major factor in stress. And exhaustion occurs when your body has used up its general adaptation energy.

After your body passes the general adaptation syndrome stages, you enter two stages of rejuvenation: recovery and replenishment. Recovery represents the end of expending energy and the beginning of recuperation. And replenishment begins the recuperation of your adaptation energy.

How to manage stress

You can manage personal stress and teach your co-workers to do so by using some commonly practiced unwinding techniques. You can practice all of these techniques at home and many, though not all, at the office. Most successful stress reduction methods involve a combination of the five senses: sight, sound, smell, taste, and touch. Techniques that can help you and your staff manage stressful situations include relaxation, meditation, environment, and exercise.

Relaxation

The most common method of dealing with stress is to take conscious steps to relax. This might involve taking a break and getting away from your desk; often it helps to eat or drink something. Even stopping long enough to take several deep breaths can help you to relax.

If there is a peaceful spot such as an atrium or garden near your work area, you could spend a few minutes there. If not, simply keeping fresh flowers on your desk could help during critical moments.

Meditation

Meditation is a more concentrated effort at controlling stress by relaxing or gaining control of body functions such as breathing. While there are several styles of meditation, most agree on the following important factors for success. Be in a quiet surrounding, preferably with lowered lighting and no interruptions. Establish a focus point – something to look at or listen to that helps you concentrate. Adopt an accepting attitude – the belief that your situation is manageable and you are okay. Find a comfortable position, either seated or prone.

The physical changes likely to occur during meditation include less consumption of oxygen, a decrease in the rate of breathing and pulse, lowered blood pressure, and decreased muscle tension.

Environment

The physical work environment can add to or detract from stress. If necessary, Help Desk staff should ask their manager to help solve environmental problems such as malfunctioning telephone equipment, excessive noise, or too much pedestrian traffic.

You can also improve your environment by personalizing your work areas. Most employees do this by keeping photos at their desks such as pictures of family, favorite vacations, or photo calendars. Amusing knick-knacks and humorous flyers also help reduce tension, provided they are not offensive.

Some companies supply white noise or background music in work areas. While background music can be helpful, it can also be controversial, since personal tastes are so varied.

Exercise

Many companies offer exercise facilities in their corporate environments. If your office doesn't have an exercise facility, brief walks to the break area, up a flight or two of stairs, or around your building can be helpful.

Stretching exercises at desks can also help relieve tension. Take the time to learn and practice stretching exercises best suited to counteract the time you spend on the phone or at the computer. In addition, a wooden neck roller can help you massage any stiffness out of your back and neck.

Companies that don't have their own exercise facilities often sponsor memberships in fitness clubs at reduced rates for employees. Regular exercise has a major, positive impact on health and resistance to stress.

Avoiding burnout

According to a study by the National Training & Computers Project, more than 70% of Help Desk staff members report moderate to severe levels of job burnout after 18 months on the job (*The Assist Journal*, February

1989, published by National Training & Computers Project, Raquette Lake, New York).

Burnout is undoubtedly one of the greatest dangers Help Desk agents face. The main danger of burnout is that it simply is not recognized until too late. Your Help Desk can use many methods to help reduce the likelihood of burnout including job rotations, special projects, stress management classes, recognizing superior performance, off-site training, mandatory vacations, and listening to staff suggestions.

Job rotation   Most firms rotate personnel in Help Desk responsibility areas to maintain a higher level of productivity and reduce stress. In periods of high volume, however, most available staff may be answering calls, resolving problems, or routing problems to proper support resources.

Staff members may rotate on and off phone duty. When off the phone, staff personnel are able to work in a less stressful environment, but on equally valuable tasks.

Highly technical Help Desks may rotate their Help Desk personnel in and out of technical positions for several weeks or months to allow agents time to develop and maintain their specialized skill levels.

Special projects   Providing personnel with special projects such as analyzing problem trends or developing a Help Desk newsletter or brochure gives agents time away from the phones. This supplies people with an avenue of change. Such tasks can also greatly enhance job satisfaction and pride.

Stress management classes   Numerous offerings and formats on stress management classes exist. Managers may consider making such a class mandatory for all Help Desk personnel to learn to avoid burnout.

Recognize superior performance   Managers and Help Desk agents can recognize co-workers' superior performance by increasing responsibilities, giving financial awards, establishing an employee of the month program, or providing special privileges such as close-in parking.

Off-site training   You can attend general or technical training, join customer groups, or continue your formal education.

Mandatory vacation   Everyone needs time off. Don't skip vacations or let your staff miss vacations.

Listen to staff suggestions   You and your staff can experience less burnout if you listen to everyone's suggestions and take actions where appropriate. Managers may involve staff members in all aspects of planning.

Summary

Hiring a good Help Desk team and keeping team members motivated is a key factor in Help Desk success. It's important to begin by fully communicating job descriptions, performance expectations, pay ranges, and career paths.

Regular analysis of calls received can help determine any changes needed in staff size and skill requirements, including staff development needs. To build expertise and morale, consider providing at least one week of off-site training or continuing education to all employees each year.

Stress on the job has become a serious national problem. Because Help Desk staff are always dealing with unhappy customers, they are particularly vulnerable to excess stress and burnout. In 1991, *Health Magazine* listed the job of complaint handler/customer service as the eighth most stressful job in the United States. This makes it particularly important for you to find ways to reduce stress and recognize early signs of burnout to return each staff member to a positive, productive frame of mind.

For expanded coverage on this topic, refer to Help Desk Institute's *Managing Stress, A Guide for Customer Support Professionals* by Karen Eberhardt, 1992.

chapter 5

Call handling – moments of truth

Any opportunity an organization has to form a positive or negative impression in the customer's mind is called a moment of truth. No IS organization has more moment-of-truth opportunities than the Help Desk.

The Help Desk is the first point of contact for customers with problems, therefore, the impressions you leave with customers are key to their perceptions of the IS organization – and possibly of the entire company.

Impressions are often based less on what you say and more on how you say it. Therefore, this chapter emphasizes how to manage those critical interactions. First, we'll focus on basic telephone skills including how your equipment and tone of voice can impact your customer service. We'll also provide tips on smoothing your interactions with your customers as well as how to listen more effectively.

Next, we'll discuss customer relationships, starting with understanding customers' needs and developing the art of negotiation. Finally, we'll discuss how to recognize and manage customer behavior including passive and aggresive behaviors.

Basic telephone skills

The telephone skills you need at the Help Desk encompass using the telephone equipment, controlling your tone of voice, interacting with your customers on a professional basis, and learning to listen – really listen – to your customers.

Using the equipment

Agents should be comfortable with their telephone equipment. Be sure you can easily transfer calls, place calls on hold, and set up conference calls, if these functions are available. Practice using these functions before you need them.

Answer the phone in as few rings as practical. You may program the telephone equipment to automatically forward calls after a certain number of rings, such as the third ring.

When using the telephone, position the mouthpiece directly in front of your mouth. Using telephone headsets ensures correct placement of the mouthpiece while freeing the agent's hands and neck. Speaking on a telephone requires better articulation than face-to-face conversations, where some communication is visual.

You may have telephone equipment that allows the customer to listen to music or a radio station while waiting. While this can ease the stress of waiting, it's

---

1. Energy
2. Rate of speech
3. Pitch

Figure 5-1   **Three factors that primarily control voice quality**

better to give customers information regarding current average hold times, so they can anticipate the delay.

Be sure to place the caller on hold before discussing the customer's problem with someone else. It's not sufficient to cover the mouthpiece with your hand. Customers may still hear a conversation at the other end of the line.

If you are eating or drinking something when the telephone rings, swallow and wait a few seconds before answering.

Tone of voice

The inflection in your voice is important. It can convey sincerity, humor, sarcasm, and skepticism as well as many other shades of meaning. Make sure you communicate what you intend.

Figure 5-1 presents the three factors that primarily control the quality of voice you project: energy, rate of speech, pitch. Your energy level reflects attitude and enthusiasm. Your rate of speech needs to be at a moderate level – normally about 125 words per minute. Faster speaking may create problems, and speaking too slowly can convey the impression of patronizing the customer. And you can vary the pitch of your voice by modulating your tone and inflection.

If you smile when answering the telephone, your voice will actually sound friendlier. This can have a big impact on how the customer feels about you and the Help Desk.

Customer contact

You may never meet many of your customers face to face; you'll know them only through the telephone. After greeting the caller, identify your department's name and yourself, unless your company has a policy against this.

Suggested greeting: "Good afternoon. This is the Help Desk, Mary speaking. How can I help you?"

Note the person's name and use it in the conversation. Different customs prevail at different companies and countries, but in general, use first names to personalize the conversation and hold the customer's attention. However, don't be too informal. Also, be consistent – establish a policy at your Help Desk, so all agents follow the same guidelines.

If you need to place a customer on hold, ask for permission and wait for an answer. Never leave a person on hold for more than 30 to 60 seconds without checking back.

Keep track of who is holding on each line. Avoid questions such as, "Who were you holding for?" Other statements to avoid include: "I don't know where Steven is, but I'll have him call you when he gets back," and "She is in the middle of a big problem right now." These statements tell customers two negative things: Their problems are not perceived as big, and they must wait in line for Help Desk agents to solve other problems first.

You should be able to access basic information related to the customer very quickly. Ideally this customer information would be on a PC or mainframe database. Or, it could be as simple as a box of index cards or a Rolodex file with basic information recorded on the cards. Quick access is important, but maintaining thorough, current information is also critical. For this reason, it is vastly preferable to get beyond paper-based systems – which are difficult to update – and onto a computerized system that automatically updates information as your organization makes network and configuration changes.

If your Help Desk is not staffed 24 hours a day, you should still have someone, such as a computer operator, provide coverage in off hours. You should also have a method for determining which calls are for the Help Desk. In addition, the person covering the calls should conform as much as possible to the guidelines and techniques the regular staff uses.

Learning to listen

Listen carefully; this sounds obvious, but it's still the most important lesson for agents to learn. If you don't listen carefully, you will hear what you expect to hear. Callers will pick up on this and your credibility will be lost. Although it can be an important time-saver to identify repeat problems with similar solutions, each problem has the potential of being unique. Ask specific questions to separate the unusual from the routine.

Once you document the details of a problem, affirm the importance of the problem to the caller. For example, use the caller's words whenever possible. ("I understand that not receiving that information is delaying the completion of your weekly report. We'll try to find out what happened as quickly as possible.")

Other conversation tips

You can also improve your telephone techniques by using open-ended and close-ended questions, getting expert help you necessary, ending your conversations by getting agreement from your customers, and making follow-up calls to certain customers when necessary.

Question styles   When you want to encourage customers to speak freely, use open-ended questions – questions they can't answer with a yes or no. For example, instead of asking, "Has this problem negatively impacted your area?" ask, "How would you describe the impact of this problem on your area?"

When you want to limit the range of customers' responses to a choice among alternatives, use close-ended questions. For example, "We can get someone there quickly. Will 2:00 this afternoon be OK?"

You often need to use open-ended questions at the start of a call to learn the necessary details. These questions usually start with these words: who, what, when, where, why, and how.

Close-ended questions can help you gain agreement and limit the length of a conversation. They often start with these words: did, can, have, do, is, will, and would.

Getting additional help   Don't refer customers to second-level support personnel. Agents should contact those persons directly or confer with them. Customers will become frustrated if they are referred to a second and third person, especially if they can't reach them immediately or if they reach the wrong person. This also creates another problem – customers will learn to bypass your Help Desk and call the "experts" directly, defeating the purpose of the Help Desk.

Ending the conversation   Conversations can often take many paths and can become confusing when it comes to what is expected of whom. At the end of your conversation, briefly summarize the problem, the planned actions, and the timing of those actions. This ensures both parties agree and understand each other.

Tell the customer the reference number you assign to the problem, and encourage the customer to make a note of it. It will save both parties time during future discussions about the problem.

Always thank customers for calling and encourage them to call again if any more problems occur. The customer will remember the end of the conversation more than any other segment. Let the customer hang up first; this gives the customer a final chance to say something.

Follow-up Whatever follow-up actions you commit to, it's critical you document these actions in the call record and then carry out these actions. This is particularly important with promised call-backs, since customers often have to wait in queue to reach an agent and will resent explaining the situation again to a new person.

In many cases, agents will have dispatched a service technician as the follow-up action to a call. In that case, it is the agent's responsibility to track vendors or service partners to ensure they reach the site as promised and work within service guidelines. Realistically, this is often difficult, but it must be accomplished in some fashion – even after the fact, if necessary – since the customer has no point of accountability other than the Help Desk.

Customer relationships

Vanderbilt University coach Red Sanders is attributed with saying, "Winning isn't everything, it's the only thing." Similarly, customer service is the only thing for the Help Desk; it has no other reason to exist. Serving your customers means making them feel good about moment-of-truth transactions. Beyond the basics of call handling, the Help Desk must strive to build a rapport with its customer community. The Help Desk builds a reputation over time. If that reputation is less than satisfactory, it will take time to change it, but it can certainly be done.

Some key areas to focus on when building customer relations include understanding customers' needs, creating a customer liaison, the art of negotiation, recognizing and managing customer behavior, and accentuating the positive.

Understanding customers' needs

Your agents should know as much about your customers as practical. For internal customers, this includes having access to information about customers' organizations and operating hours as well as specific configuration information about their sites and workstations. You can keep this information on paper or in the computer, but you can more easily update it if you keep it on-line. This information is even more useful if you can integrate it into your problem management system.

In addition, experienced Help Desk personnel know their customers' psychological needs. A particular customer service center, for example, may run several different applications. Losing several of those applications wouldn't make them happy, but it may not threaten their basic business. One particular application, however, might be absolutely critical – especially between noon and 5:00 p.m. on Fridays. Understanding these differences can make the difference in how customers perceive your Help Desk.

Even for Help Desks serving external customers, it is possible to build a database of customer information that can help the service process. This is often accomplished through the use of warranty or registration cards. Anything helps, since it is always pleasing to customers when the agent recognizes them and knows something about their situation from the beginning.

Some form of caller identification can also help in this process. Although the caller ID promoted by telephone companies has limited use so far, Help Desks can use simple techniques such as combining dedicated telephone service lines for selected areas with telephone displays to identify the caller's region. In more sophisticated systems, a voice response unit (VRU) can prompt the customer to enter a unique ID over the telephone before the call is turned over to an agent. Any unique identifier can accomplish this such as a Social Security number, device number, or personal identification number (PIN). Agents can then be prompted with relevant information about customers before they have said a word.

The customer liaison

Some internal Help Desks in large organizations designate individuals to represent the interests of large customer bases within or outside the IS organization. This person is usually called the customer liaison. We can't overemphasize the importance of maintaining effective relationships with these individuals. In some cases, customer liaisons are active and visible, while in others they will go about their normal, day-to-day functions, only calling Help Desk management if they're having problems.

Whatever style the customer liaisons follow, it is critical you make yourself and your Help Desk visible to them. They often know about problems with your services that you don't. They may not seek you out to tell you – trying to be nice – but you need to be aware of these problems to resolve them before they boil over. A strong working relationship with these individuals can also help protect the Help Desk against undue criticism during problem times. In many cases, how well your Help Desk performs is less important than how these representatives feel about the job you're doing. Also, these representatives often will have your boss's ear.

The art of negotiation

Help Desk call handling presents many situations in which you need to negotiate with the customer. Negotiating involves recognizing the needs of the customer, comparing these needs with your organization's ability to deliver what is required, then reaching a compromise that satisfies both parties.

When handling calls, you may encounter a customer making an unreasonable demand or expecting a response quicker than the priority of the problem warrants. Use open questions to determine why the customer is acting in this manner. You might find a hidden problem the Help Desk or the customer needs to address.

When you have assessed the situation and decided on a course of action, it's important to be direct and specific in your statements. With some customers, you'll need to be assertive. If the customer is still unwilling to accept the situation, refer the problem to a supervisor. At all times, you need to remain positive and service oriented.

How to recognize
and manage customer behavior

Every customer is different. Agents should learn to recognize these differences and adjust their behavior accordingly. This section addresses different techniques for dealing with difficult customers. While difficult customers present your staff with exceptional challenges, they represent opportunities to demonstrate skills, fix problems, and develop or rebuild customer relationships.

To understand difficult customers you must first understand the three basic communication behaviors. These behaviors are passive, aggressive, and assertive.

Passive behavior   On the surface, passive people seem easy to work with. They usually appear agreeable and hide other feelings. However, they generally have a great deal of stress because they seldom get what they want. They let others walk all over them. Passive people usually remain passive only so long. Often, they become adept at blocking or even sabotaging others' efforts without taking responsibility for their actions. Because they have not made their own desires or needs clear, it is difficult to negotiate with them. This often results in frustration and surprises for those dealing with them.

Passive customers can be difficult to recognize, since they are apparently so agreeable. If a customer's behavior strikes you as more timid or accommodating than the severity of their problem warrants, you may be dealing with a passive customer. The key to managing passive customers is attempting to draw them out by asking open-ended questions. Make sure you clarify the impact of the problem, since these customers may understate the severity of the problem. Double-check any agreements you make with these customers to ensure they agree with the resolution and are not just being nice.

Aggressive behavior   Aggressive people are capable of expressing their own feelings and needs, but do so in a way that violates the rights of others. Aggressive behaviors include blaming, threatening, humiliating, and dominating. Aggressive people are difficult because they care nothing about others' rights. They always seem to get their way but also have a lot of stress, because they are always involved in conflict.

Aggressive customers are easy to recognize by their bullying tactics. In dealing with this type of person, it's important not to react emotionally to their behavior. Don't become defiant or unhelpful – either in a direct confrontation or passive/aggressively. And don't give in to their unreasonable demands.

How do you deal with aggressive customers? First, actively acknowledge and empathize with their problems to cool down these people. Second, if you can satisfy their requests by normal processes, do it, regardless of these customers' behavior. If not, explain what you can and can't do and why. Attempt to secure some sort of agreement through close-ended questions. If the customers are still unsatisfied, refer the call to the Help Desk supervisor, before the your patience becomes exhausted.

Assertive behavior   Assertive people know and respect their own rights as well as the rights of others. Assertive behavior increases the chances of a good compromise or satisfactory result without making others angry. No one's life is stress free, but assertive people generally have less stress and find what stress they do have to be manageable.

Although assertive customers usually will be more demanding than passive customers, in the long run, your agents will learn to appreciate their directness and willingness to compromise. Also, assertive customers always present the fewest unpleasant surprises to both agents and Help Desk managers.

Managing angry customers   We all get angry from time to time, regardless of our basic communication style, and Help Desk staff are often faced with customers who are intensely frustrated. At the start of the call, angry customers will always seem aggressive to the agent; as these customers cool off they will usually drop back into their normal style of communication. The following guidelines help agents deal with angry or frustrated callers.

Prepare yourself. Take a deep breath and be prepared to listen to your customer's angry words without taking them personally. Try to keep a pleasant attitude in your mind and in your voice.

Let your customer vent the anger. Don't interrupt, even if you know how to solve the problem. These customers aren't prepared to listen until they've finished getting it "off their chests."

Listen and take notes. Write down your customer's exact words as well as you can.

Refer to your notes to paraphrase what the customer said to make sure you understand the situation. Be sure to communicate to the customer that you were listening.

Empathize with the customer. Say something like, "I understand how this could be frustrating. We'll find a solution together." This preserves your customer's dignity and usually defuses the anger.

Ask, "What would you like for a solution?" If the request is workable, do it; if not, look for alternatives. Explain what can and can't be done and, if possible, offer options to the customer. This makes your customer an owner of the solution.

Get agreement. Verify your customer's under-standing and acceptance of the solution.

Take care of yourself. After particularly stressful calls, it's important to take a few seconds to take a deep breath and let the physical effects of the stress wear off. Check yourself to make sure you've calmed down before taking another call.

Tips for building customer relationships

Admit when you don't know the answer to a customer's problem. It is far better to say, "I don't know, but I'll find out" than to pretend knowing the answer but be unable to explain it.

If you give a customer an answer you later realize was wrong, contact the customer as soon as practical. The customer will be happier to learn the correct answer now, than encounter further problems later.

Avoid getting too casual with a customer, even if you have worked with the person many times. Don't eat or drink while on the telephone or use buzz words or data processing terms unfamiliar to the customer.

Be sure to acknowledge the importance of the problem to the customer. Paraphrase the nature of the problem as well as its importance to make sure you understand the situation. Never imply that a customer's problem is "no big deal."

If you follow up a problem for a customer, return the call within an agreed-upon period of time, such as one hour. This is important even if you only let the customer know you're still addressing the problem. If the customer does not answer the phone, leave a message stating the current status. If there is no way to leave a message use electronic mail, if available.

Periodically review the problems or questions initiated by specific customers. If questions are repetitively about the same software, you might suggest the customer take a class, or you might need to notify the software maintenance team if a design problem is involved. If the calls involve repetitive hardware problems, bring this to the attention of someone in hardware maintenance. The ability to catch problems like this depends on two procedures: regularly reviewing problems and properly logging all calls.

Accentuate the positive

Agents' attitudes are key to the Help Desk's success. The staff's general morale and attitude will be reflected in how they treat their customers. Managers have more impact on this positive environment than they realize.

1. Give a simple, public thank you for work well done.
2. Recognize special contributions.
3. Provide free snacks or drinks.
4. Host an after-hours dinner or party.
5. Promote the best performers.
6. Get special thanks from a senior manager in the company.

Figure 5-2 **Six ideas for promoting healthy attitudes at the Help Desk**

The most important aspect is the manager's attitude. If a manager is calm, supportive, strongly oriented toward customer service, and a good listener, then the Help Desk will ultimately reflect those qualities. A good rule of thumb is to ask staff to treat each other the same way they are expected to treat their customers. This goes for managers, too.

Managers also need to be sensitive to periods when Help Desk stress levels are particularly high. This is an opportunity to show real leadership by finding ways to relieve the pressure.

Figure 5-2 presents some approaches for keeping attitudes healthy at your Help Desk. These approaches include giving a public thank you for work well done, recognizing special contributions, providing free snacks or drinks, hosting an after-hours dinner or party, getting special thanks from a senior manager in the company, and promoting the best performers.

Finally, humor is the greatest stress release for us all. You need to use it carefully, however, since ill-placed humor can easily offend. The safest and best-appreciated humor is to poke fun at oneself. This can be especially effective when senior managers are willing to allow harmless jokes at their own expense.

For a more thorough treatment on the topic of customer relationships, refer to Help Desk Institute's self-study course *Customer Service Skills for Help Desk Professionals.*

chapter **6**

Call handling tools

Although a small Help Desk can perform basic functions with only a few telephones and trained staff, most Help Desks face increasing demands for higher productivity and better customer service.

In this chapter, we'll dicuss the commonly used systems for handling calls while making the best use of staff resources. We'll also cover phone systems and features, problem documentation, and problem management systems.

Phone systems and features for capturing calls

Methods for recording problems and initial diagnoses are determined by how the Help Desk receives calls and the systems used to record and track problems.

1. Message capabilities when all lines are busy
2. Uniform call distributors (UCD)
3. Auto attendant features (AAF)
4. Automatic call sequencers (ACS)
5. Automatic call distributors (ACD)
6. Voice response units (VRU)

Figure 6-1   **Six phone system options to consider**

Help Desks receive calls through voice mail, direct customer access to problem management systems, electronic mail, a staffed message center, and walk-up access – as well as through the ordinary telephone call.

The telephone equipment you choose for the Help Desk is extremely important. The instruments and systems should be of sufficient quality to stand up to constant use.

Figure 6-1 presents some of the phone system options available. When choosing phone systems, consider headsets versus handsets, message and recording capabilities, automatic call sequencers, uniform call distributors, automatic call distributors, auto attendant features, and voice response units. We discuss these system options in more detail in the following paragraphs.

Whichever phone system tools you use, getting the most out of them requires providing training for primary staff members and some training for backup individuals.

1. Incoming calls
2. Outbound calls
3. Available agent time
4. Calls delayed
5. Time on hold
6. Calls abandoned
7. Calls transferred
8. Conference calls
9. Call duration

Figure 6-2   **Nine elements an automatic call distributor can track**

Automatic call sequencer

An automatic call sequencer (ACS) is typically a device attached in front of the key or private branch exchange (PBX) system. The telephone circuits coming to the call center are attached to this device. The ACS answers the call, plays an announcement and possibly also plays music. The ACS also alerts the agent to the presence of the call and indicates the length of hold through varying lamp flashing sequences. This way, the responder can answer the oldest call first by picking up that line. The big issue with ACS devices is that they are passive; the responder must initiate the answer.

Uniform call distributor

The uniform call distributor (UCD) provides top-down or round-robin call routing. The UCD follows a predetermined form of call routing that typically cannot deviate. It tends to be less expensive and more rudimentary than an automatic call distribution system (discussed below), but may be perfectly acceptable, depending on the appli-

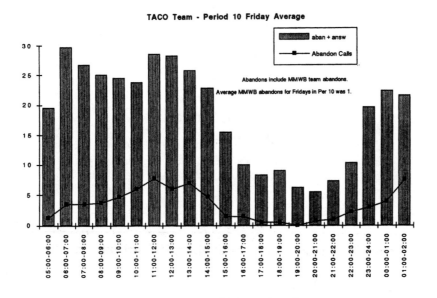

TACO Team - Period 10 Friday Average

Figure 6-3   ACD statistics showing calls received and calls abandoned by hour

cation. The UCD has operational and management information limitations: The distribution is biased to a small portion of the responder group, namely those at the top of the list. Those at the bottom of the list may have other primary responsibilities.

Automatic call distributor

The Automatic Call Distributor (ACD) allows call queuing on dedicated lines on a first-in, first-out basis. One line at a time is connected to an initial recorded message, then transferred on queue to some form of broadcast message all on-hold callers hear. The ACD ensures the call in queue the longest is answered first.

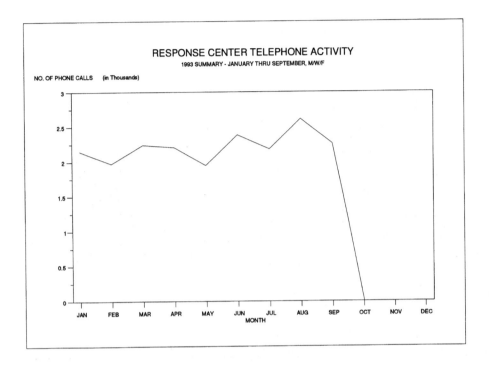

RESPONSE CENTER TELEPHONE ACTIVITY
1993 SUMMARY - JANUARY THRU SEPTEMBER, M/W/F

Figure 6-4   ACD statistics showing number of call received by month

An ACD typically delivers the call with no decision required from the responder. The cost of an ACD has declined as more products have entered the market. Your organization may already have this system, which could be expanded to include the Help Desk, if you are not currently using these features.

An ACD has substantial processing and memory capacity. Typically, an ACD routes the call to the responder who has been idle longest (but this is programmable) and tends to equalize the workload across all responders. The ACD maintains a "free list" of available responders. You also can program the ACD to distribute calls exactly like a UCD.

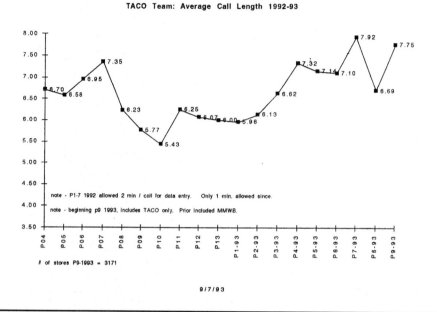

Figure 6-5   ACD statistics showing average call length

Many ACDs also allow conditional call routing for interrupt-routing based on a service, time, or traffic-load condition. This causes the call routing to better reflect the business application.

Figure 6-2 presents a suggested list of telephone statistics Help Desks can capture using an ACD.

Auto attendant feature

ACDs can have auto attendant features or announce-ment devices that provide prerecorded announcements to an incoming caller. These devices come in two forms – a mechanical continuous loop and a solid-state digital unit. A digital device is preferable due to sound fidelity, instant reset, replay, and reliability advantages.

A mechanical continuous loop runs at a constant tape speed and continuously plays a prerecorded message. If

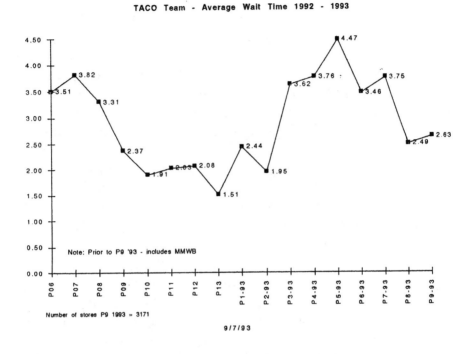

TACO Team - Average Wait Time 1992 - 1993

Note: Prior to P9 '93 - includes MMWB

Number of stores P9 1993 = 3171

9/7/93

Figure 6-6   ACD statistics showing average wait times

a call arrives one second after the beginning of a 10-second message, the caller will hear a nine-second pause, then hears the start of the message.

Most systems now use solid-state announcers that eliminate recording degradation problems induced by wear on the moving tape and playback heads. Digital announcers are more reliable, because they have no moving parts.

Some auto attendants now have capabilities of voice response units as well. They can offer the caller a selection menu and route the call to a different phone split based on that selection.

Voice response unit

A voice response unit (VRU) is normally used in conjunction with an automatic call distributor. Like the ACD, it offers the caller a selection menu, but there the similarity ends. The VRU is a computer that can hold an extended dialog with customers over their telephones by capturing information from the telephone keypad and acting upon it. The Help Desk can use a VRU to present information to the agent before the agent has spoken to the customer. In many cases, it can interface directly with a host computer to provide total service to the customer for simple transactions such as account balance information and terminal and printer resets. Successfully answering calls without agent involvement is a main automation goal of many Help Desk managers.

The principle drawback of VRUs for application processing is that it is time consuming and awkward for customers to enter alphabetical data on a telephone keypad. Newer VRUs have a voice recognition feature that could help resolve this problem; however, its use in Help Desks is not extensive yet.

Broadcasts to delayed callers

Callers are less likely to disconnect while on hold if they receive some feedback that confirms they are in the queue. This can be accomplished by announcements and playing music or a radio station during the delay. You can alter the message to inform callers of a known large-scale problem, which may be the reason for the call. If that's the case, then the caller will likely disconnect.

Recently the American Society of Composers and Publishers (ASCAP) has attempted to levy royalty fees against organizations that use music on hold. They contend this is a rebroadcast of copyrighted material. This has encouraged companies to use promotional or

STAFFING CALCULATIONS

Press alt-I to look up analyst
Press alt-i to import new acd data
ASA 210

Press alt-p to print
Press alt-k to look up ASA given
specific number of analysts

TIME		AVE CALLS	TOTAL WORKLOAD	ERLANGS	AVG HANDLE TIME/PERIOD	DP*DF	ANALYSTS NEEDED	ANALYSTS AVAILABLE	RESULTING ASA	DP*DF
7	30	2.57	1774	0.99	690.00	0.30434783	2	4	9.11	0.013209
8	0	7.86	5421	3.01	690.00	0.30434783	4	4	9.11	0.013209
8	30	10.14	6999	3.89	690.00	0.30434783	5	6	7.67	0.01112
9	0	14.43	9956	5.53	690.00	0.30434783	7	6	16.20	0.023475
9	30	15.57	10744	5.97	690.00	0.30434783	7	7	12.85	0.018626
10	0	6.00	4140	2.30	690.00	0.30434783	3	7	6.56	0.0095
10	30	3.29	2267	1.26	690.00	0.30434783	3	7	6.56	0.0095
11	0	20.86	14391	8.00	690.00	0.30434783	10	8	10.18	0.01475
11	30	17.71	12223	6.79	690.00	0.30434783	10	8	13.61	0.019725
12	0	15.71	10843	6.02	690.00	0.30434783	8	7	12.85	0.018626
12	30	15.71	10843	6.02	690.00	0.30434783	9	7	6.56	0.0095
13	0	18.43	12716	7.06	690.00	0.30434783	9	7	12.85	0.018626
13	30	15.71	10843	6.02	690.00	0.30434783	7	7	12.85	0.018626
14	0	17.29	11927	6.63	690.00	0.30434783	9	7	6.56	0.0095
14	30	19.29	13307	7.39	690.00	0.30434783	10	7	12.85	0.018626
15	0	17.43	12026	6.68	690.00	0.30434783	8	8	10.18	0.01475
15	30	18.00	12420	6.90	690.00	0.30434783	9	7	17.45	0.025284
16	0	16.57	11434	6.35	690.00	0.30434783	7	6	16.20	0.023475
16	30	9.71	6703	3.72	690.00	0.30434783	5	6	7.67	0.01112
17	0	8.86	6111	3.40	690.00	0.30434783	5	5	5.27	0.007644
17	30	4.14	2859	1.59	690.00	0.30434783	3	4	4.60	0.00666
18	0	1.57	1084	0.60	690.00	0.30434783	1	3	7.19	0.010425
TOTALS		276.86					141.00		10.22	

** This is a spreadsheet that automates our staffing level calculations. ACD information is save in an ascii format and imported into this lotus spreadsheet. We can then run a macro that will lookup the number of analysts needed for each 1/2 hour period. We can also estimate the Average Speed of Answer given the number of analysts available for a given period.

10/12/93

Figure 6-7   ACD statistics can be loaded in a spreadsheet to calculate optimum staffing levels.

all-news formats. However, you may still have a problem if the station plays commercials during the broadcast that contain copyrighted music.

Call routing tables

Different manufacturers refer to call routing tables by different names: call control table, ACD call routing, call vector or routing table. A call processing table is a set of preprogrammed steps residing in the ACD system memory. These may be a standard set of steps, programmed into the machine before installation, or the customer may change the steps to address particular call processing demands as they occur. Although all call routing tables appear similar, they are filled with important nuances and subtleties.

The capabilities of call routing tables are the core of call center management. For example, suppose you are introducing a new service into your Help Desk that a new customer base uses. This was a top-priority project by senior management with very short lead times, so only a few of your agents are thoroughly trained in the new application; the rest have had some basic training, so they know what it's about, but not how to fix it. You've programmed this new application as a separate selection on your auto attendant, but this is where the fun begins.

Of course, you program your routing tables to attempt to route this "split" to the trained agents, but suppose they're all busy. Do you overflow the calls to the other agents, or have the callers wait on hold until the trained agents are free? Call volumes for this new service are not expected to be high, but proper servicing is critical. Do you let these trained agents take other types of calls as well, risking these new calls sitting on hold or going to a less-qualified agent? This just skims the surface of decisions regarding routing tables, but you get the idea of the complexities involved.

Here's an additional fact to consider in routing tables: Unless you have the staffing luxury of completely segregating calls into different staff groups, during peak calling periods all your primary routing decisions will be washed away by the "everybody's busy" effect, and calls will go to the agent who is free first, despite your best planning attempts.

Call monitoring statistics

One of the primary benefits of an ACD is information generation. You can display call monitoring statistics in reports or graphs. Graphical representation of the data, especially if it uses color, allows more efficient communication, because trends and exceptions are easier to spot. Color graphs are often used for high-level managers who have limited time to analyze the information.

Local terminals or wall-mounted electronic display units are frequently used for real-time monitoring of queues to ensure the highest quality of service. When hold times lengthen, managers may have additional staff they can assign to the phones.

Figures 6-3 through 6-7 show how Help Desks can format ACD data into reports. All telephone equipment statistics should be available in total and also by shift or specific time intervals, such as every 30 minutes. Most Help Desks analyze statistical information by extension and summarize such as incoming calls, outbound calls, available agent time, calls delayed, time on hold, calls abandoned, calls transferred, conference calls, and call duration.

Tips for using call management systems

The variety and sophistication of call management systems is growing by leaps and bounds and their usage is growing just as explosively. It's rare today to call a major department store or airline without first being asked to select options from a menu. While these systems have enormous potential to improve Help Desk productivity, it's also important to consider their impact on customer service.

A more productive Help Desk is not automatically a better Help Desk from the customer's point of view. Horror stories of getting lost in a voice response unit menu are common, as are the frustrations of perceived barriers to speaking to an agent. Here are a few tips to ensure your customers won't get turned off by your new technology.

To the extent possible, always let your customers know in advance of changes to call handling procedures. Give them the list of the new menu selections and the shortcuts for commonly accessed applications.

Always leave an "out" in your menu selections to get to an agent and to go back to the previous menu selection. These options alone will eliminate most of the commonly experienced frustrations.

Keep your menu selections short, and list the most commonly accessed selections first to save customers' listening time. Remember, most statistics about hold times are kept from the time the customer gets in the queue, although it may take the customer a full minute or two to get there using a poorly designed auto attendant or VRU.

For several weeks after making a change in the selection menu, give a quick reminder that selections have changed early in your greeting. This helps prevent frequent callers from speed entering their old selection numbers.

Finally, call your own number, and call it often. Try different paths, and see what it feels like to be on the other end. If you haven't listened for a while, we'd be

```
1. Telephone
2. E-mail
3. In person
4. Voice mail
5. Message centers
```

Figure 6-8   The five most common methods customers use to present problems to Help Desks

surprised if you don't have a few good ideas for changes by the time you're finished.

Problem documentation for recording calls

Recording calls is an important Help Desk function. The data gathered is critical to reporting and managing problems. Many firms use a packaged automated system (typically with some modifications) to record problems. Most Help Desk personnel log calls while they are on the phone with the customers. A few only log those calls assigned outside the Help Desk or requiring further monitoring. Generally, we believe it's important to log all calls. Unrecorded calls are missed opportunities to identify problem trends, improve service, and take credit – in the form of statistics – for Help Desk problems solved.

Electronic mail and voice mail are other ways of capturing problems. Some shops have mainline problem recording systems but most often organizations use them when the Help Desk is closed or if the caller isn't able to wait for an agent on the phone. Several

1. Reference number
2. Date and time reported
3. Help Desk agent
4. Customer name, telephone number, location, and secondary contact
5. Problem description
6. Date and time assigned
7. Assignee's name
8. Priority or severity classification
9. Cross reference to other reference numbers
10. Status and completion codes
11. Hardware or software involved including serial numbers, if applicable
12. Actions taken – with dates and times (may be multiple entries)
13. Date and time agents resolved the problem
14. Resolution description

Figure 6-9   Contents of a problem report form

competing systems are available for purchase or lease, and these systems are common today for communications within companies. Mail systems are convenient, because they don't require a person at the other end to complete the communication. However, mail systems usually force Help Desks to take extra steps: the agent

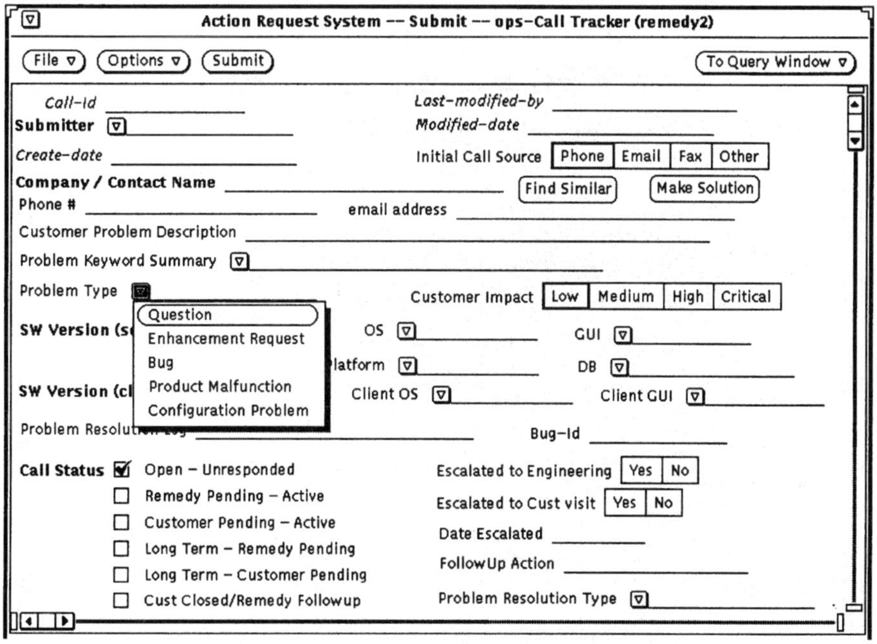

Figure 6-10   A sample problem tracking screen from a problem management system (courtesy of Remedy Corporation)

must call or mail a response, and the agent must usually transcribe the information into the problem management system.

Figure 6-8 presents the five most common methods customers use to present problems to Help Desks: telephone, E-mail, message centers, in-person, and voice mail.

Help Desks can log these problems either manually or by using automated technology.

Automated   Help Desks using automated technology log all problems (or as many as practicable) directly into a problem management system. Or the Help Desk may log problems not requiring assignment in summary form only.

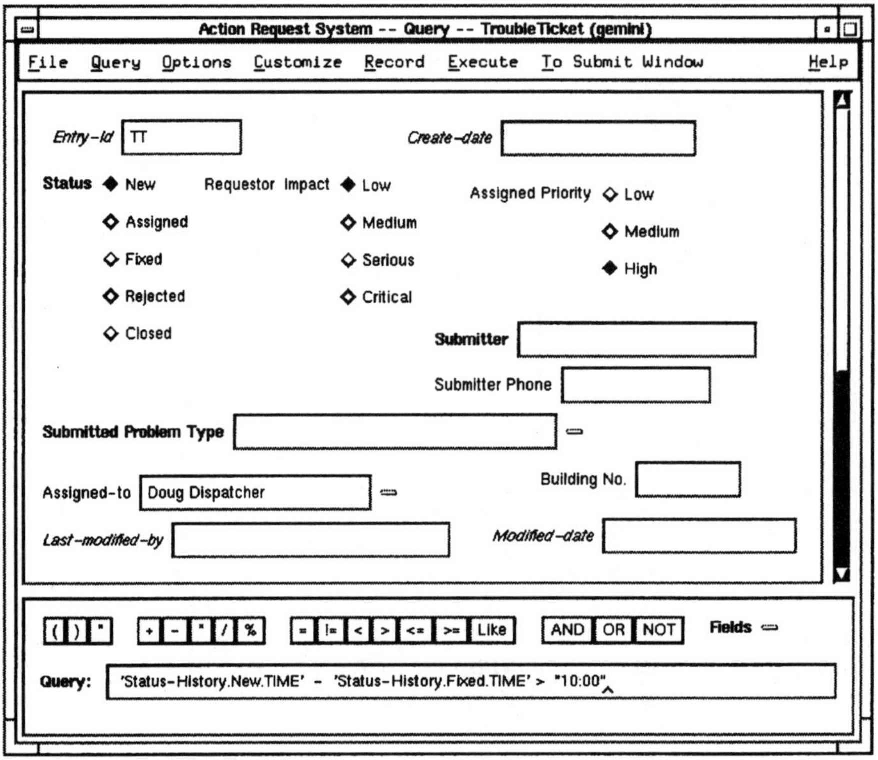

Figure 6-11   A sample trouble ticket from a problem management system (courtesy of Remedy Corporation)

It's preferable if these summary records are a designed part of the problem management system. Other shops have a separate recording method for these problems, so they capture at least some minimal data. For example, agents may touch certain numbers on a telephone keypad, so the ACD will capture the type of call and note when the problem was resolved.

Manual   Manually documenting problems involves using preprinted forms. Manual systems require manual research to gather problem trend information.

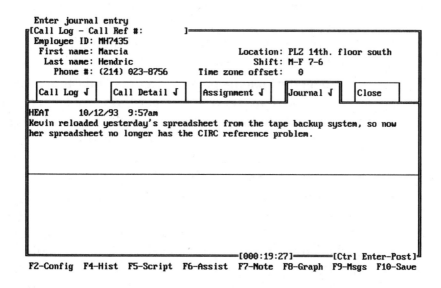

```
Enter journal entry
[Call Log - Call Ref #:          ]
 Employee ID: MH7435
   First name: Marcia                    Location: PLZ 14th. floor south
    Last name: Hendric                      Shift: M-F 7-6
     Phone #: (214) 023-8756      Time zone offset:   0

 ┌Call Log √┐  ┌Call Detail √┐  ┌Assignment √┐ ┌Journal √┐  ┌Close┐
HEAT      10/12/93  9:57am
Kevin reloaded yesterday's spreadsheet from the tape backup system, so now
her spreadsheet no longer has the CIRC reference problem.




                                     [000:19:27]        [Ctrl Enter-Post]
      F2-Config  F4-Hist  F5-Script  F6-Assist  F7-Note  F8-Graph  F9-Msgs  F10-Save
```

Figure 6-12   A journal entry screen from a problem management system (courtesy of Bendata Management Systems)

When a Help Desk uses an automated recording system, it normally sets the sequence and type of questions asked at the beginning of the call. These questions include the identity and location of the customer (terminal ID, department, and name), problem type, problem priority or severity, problem symptoms, transaction involved error codes, frequency of occurrence, descriptive text, problem history, and call back phone number. Note that these questions all precede any actual problem resolution effort. To save time for both the agent and caller, it's greatly preferable to have the system automatically pull in as much of the identification information as possible, based on some unique identifier associated with the caller or the terminal.

Most Help Desks face the question of whether to log all calls. As a rule, the higher percentage of calls you can log, the better. The tradeoff is that logging calls takes time – time agents could use to answer the next call. Nevertheless, you'll find several advantages to logging as many calls as possible.

Logged problems provide records you can use to identify problem trends and record the problems occurring in the customer community. Customers feel their problems have been better acknowledged when they know agents are logging their problems. And if a customer calls a second time, the Help Desk has a record of the previous call, helping the agent provide better service. Even logging brief calls is important to demonstrate the effective call resolution rate of the Help Desk and document the number of calls the staff actually handles

Practically speaking, few Help Desks achieve a call logging rate of 100%. Many are in the 80 to 90% range and are actively trying to improve on that. One standard of "reasonability" is to record the interaction if it doesn't take longer to record the call than to handle the call itself.

Advantages	Disadvantages
1. Generally very reliable and well-supported	1. Response times are vulnerable to other activities on the host processor and to network problems
2. Excellent for reporting and conducting any activity involving manipulating large amounts of data	2. More cumbersome to make quick fixes and enhancements and usually require extensive customization
3. Data is accessible to other applications and to management.	3. Host problems impact the Help Desk and its customers at the same time – agents may not be able to log calls at the worst times.

Figure 6-13   Advantages and disadvantages of host-based approaches

Advantages

1. Can have faster response times if designed properly and is easy to modify

2. Very flexible: can have many separate applications running concurrently that may communicate with each other

3. Functions independently of mainframe problems and offers greater application selection

Disadvantages

1. May not be networked to all support staff

2. Support roles not as well-defined

3. Batch activities such as reporting can impact response times at the agents' workstations

Figure 6-14   Advantages and disadvantages of the PC/LAN approach

The identity of the caller is readily available on most systems. Many firms use a terminal or component ID that represents the source and location of the person placing the call. In many Help Desks, agents provide the caller with a problem number to provide faster response on any callbacks and detect multiple calls on the same problem more easily. This practice helps the caller know the problem has been properly recorded and an agent is taking action.

Newer automated systems have a feature that allows fast logging of quickly resolved calls that don't require escalation. The goal is to capture some basic reporting data without slowing down the agent. Other firms support their automated systems with hard copy call sheets called "trouble tickets" or "tick sheets." These serve the same purpose. Agents complete the form during the call and later key the information into an automated system. Some firms that use hard copies have multiple part forms to allow for simplified routing during problem resolution. Other systems include a highly visible screen monitor or a white board.

By making notes on a white board (a technique employed by many Help Desks), Help Desk staff members may immediately see system conditions, even while on the phone with a customer. Highly visible screen monitors that display different systems and regions are generally found only in the larger Help Desks due to the expense and space requirements they represent. These screens sometimes include colored messages to denote levels of severity and alert Help Desk staff at a glance. Newer systems may display this information as a separate window on PCs Help Desk staff members use. This has the advantage of being visible regardless of the agent's position in the room.

Figure 6-9 presents suggested contents for a problem report form. Some of these contents include customer information, the problem description, priority classification, actions taken, status and completion codes, the date and time agents resolved the problem, and the resolution description.

Problem management systems

Most Help Desks use one of three types of problem management systems: host-based, PC/LAN-based, or a combination of Host and PC/LAN. Figures 6-10 through 6-12 show various screens from problem management systems.

Host-based systems These systems involve terminals connected through a telecommunications network to a central processor that may be local or remotely located.

PC/LAN-based systems These have individual PCs for agents connected to a central file server on the LAN. A variant on this is having PCs or terminals connected to a central minicomputer acting as a file server.

The combined system approach has two main variations. The first has calls logged locally on a PC/LAN file server arrangement but with periodic uploads to a mainframe for archival and easier data manipulation for reporting. The second approach involves a PC application interacting with a host application on a real-time basis. The PC application does much of the formatting and editing work to off load some work from the host and improve response time for the agent. The host provides that actual data base for problem records. Usually, the PC program can do some limited stand-in processing in case of host failure.

Figures 6-13 and 6-14 detail the advantages and disadvantages of the PC/LAN and host-based approaches. We didn't analyze the combination designs, since they are too varied to make generalizations. Note that the trade-offs detailed in the table apply to other Help Desk systems such as expert systems for problem analysis, documentation storage systems, and integrated systems.

1. Centralized database and rapid response time
2. Networking/multiple customer capability
3. Automatic reference number generation
4. Automatic fill of fields (date, time, customer department, location)
5. Quick reference to customer profiles
6. Calculation of elapsed times and deadlines
7. Automatic escalation of priorities
8. Data validation and range checking
9. Keyword search capability
10. Historic search and retrieval capability
11. Sort and report functions, such as all unresolved problems and overdue deadlines
12. Statistical summary reports and graphs
13. Transaction backup and recovery capabilities
14. File and field security

Figure 6-15   Fourteen common features of problem management systems

Important features

Several problem management systems are available on the market. Regardless of the type of system you choose, most systems have helpful, standard features in common. Figure 6-15 presents many of the common problem management system features now available. Some of these features include a centralized database, rapid response time, automatic fill of fields such as customer name, automatic escalation of priorities, keyword search capability, sort and report functions, and file and field security.

For a list of available systems, features, company names, and contact names, refer to Help Desk Institute's *Help Desk Buyer's Guide*.

System administration

Only one person – often the department manager – should be accountable for the problem management software system. Specific tasks related to the system include filing and updating the documentation, evaluating new releases and versions, and handling file backup and off-site storage. Other tasks include overseeing periodic data consolidation and removal, initiating statistical reports, supervising vendor contact and negotiations, and reviewing problem documentation and resolution.

chapter **7**

Call handling techniques

How can you quickly and accurately diagnose and resolve problems? This chapter presents techniques to gather complete information regarding your customers' problems, then prioritize these problems, own them even after you've assigned them, and follow-up the resolutions whenever necessary.

Initial problem diagnosis

During initial problem diagnosis, the Help Desk agent typically bases the initial diagnosis on problem symptoms and reports the diagnosis in the form of predefined problem classification codes.

1. Problem type key words
2. Component key item
3. Affected application
4. Region transaction
5. Network and mainframe
6. Customer identification and location
7. Transaction
8. Priority/severity
9. Error codes
10. Category and cause
11. Job number, if applicable
12. Step number, if applicable

Figure 7-1   **Information to identify with problem classification codes**

Figure 7-1 details information Help Desks often identify with problem classification codes. Some of these codes include problem type key words, the affected application, network or mainframe, customer information, priority, error codes, cause, and job number.

It's important that Help Desk staff and second-level support groups understand these code types and acceptable values. Besides the predefined codes, most systems have a free-form narrative area where you can document relevant descriptions for later problem analysis.

Many Help Desks handle calls received in a question and answer format, guiding the customer to supply the information necessary for problem resolution or assignment. Some Help Desk agents review checklists with customers and can diagnose and resolve most procedural problems. Help Desks develop standard checklists by problem type, application, and equipment.

Help Desks have reported good results from handling the beginning portion of each call as an open-ended question, allowing the customer to talk freely. Agents then ask close-ended questions to gain specific information. Open-ended questions at the start of calls provide customers the opportunities to vent any frustrations and express their thoughts about the problems and possible resolutions. You can then further clarify customers' problems by rephrasing or repeating them.

The appropriate method for initial problem diagnosis is determined by the knowledge or skill level of the Help Desk agent. To aid in the initial diagnosis, ask the customer about any error codes or messages displayed. One effective technique for gathering information at this stage is to explain to customers the relevance of the information requested. This helps customers become more knowledgeable and better use the Help Desk's services in the future.

Help Desks can enhance initial diagnosis by using an automated system to provide on-line access to problem history. Some systems have problem files containing the number of problems that have occurred by device, by location and in total for the previous week. If multiple occurrences of problems by device or location develop, the Help Desk can consider each problem and alert personnel to the need for permanent resolution.

Effective Help Desk systems provide historical, attached-to-device (configuration), network availability, and change information as the agent records the call.

Questions to consider

We've developed some questions for you to consider when evaluating your Help Desk's diagnostic techniques.

What information is available to your agents from your system? Do you have the caller's hardware configuration? Problem history?

Do your agents have current information from a change management system? Have the programs or hardware been changed recently? Has the data center had any change in its operating environment?

What are the recognizable symptoms of the problem? Are others in the caller's area affected by the problem? Are there any system-wide problems? Is there any reference material indicating possible solutions based on known symptoms?

Is there a code associated with the problem? Are there any messages displayed associated with a particular application or a particular software package?

Do you have computer software available to your agents to help them diagnose and analyze the problem? Has the program been updated with current information and methods of detecting known problems?

Is there anything different about the input to the customer's system? Is the volume of data higher than in the past?

Setting priorities

One of the measures of a good manager is the ability to distinguish the important from the urgent. And just because something is urgent does not necessarily mean you should work on it at once. The same is true of a good problem management system and the processes that run it. Prioritizing actions ensures your Help Desk uses its resources in the most effective manner.

One method of setting a priority is to determine the number of impacted customers and establish whether the customers can work around the problem. Many organizations set priorities based on the estimated dollar impact and the number of customers affected. Today, it's

Level	Definition	Expected Response
Severity 1	Production is down for a large number of customers and work cannot continue until the problem is fixed.	All parties including vendors are expected to work continuously (including nights and weekends) until the problem is resolved.
Severity 2	Tremendous inconvenience to customers – but a temporary circumvention or "work around" is in place.	Work is expected to continue on a workday basis until a more permanent solution is in place.
Severity 3	Mild inconvenience – a smaller customer base or a milder problem	Resolution is worked into a planned project list and scheduled.
Severity 4	More minor still	Resolution can be deferred until time allows, but should be fixed eventually.
Severity 5	Trivial	Deferred indefinitely unless something causes the perception of its importance to change, at which time the Help Desk will raise the severity level

Figure 7-2   **A sample method of qualifying severity codes**

common for the customer to help establish ground rules for setting priorities. Then, during an actual problem, the customer can assist the Help Desk agent in appropriately defining the problem's priority.

You can assign priority levels to problems. Figure 7-2 shows one system, originally developed by IBM. This system uses a severity numbering system of 1 through 5,

Priority	Expected arrival
Priority level 1	Immediately
Priority level 2	Two hours
Priority level 3	Next day
Priority level 4	Three days
Priority level 5	No special trip – next visit

Figure 7-3   An example of expected arrival times of five priority levels

1 being the most severe. In this system, documentation changes often fall into the severity 3 category.

Figure 7-3 presents an approach for setting priorities by defining time limits for the arrival of a response team. This approach is particularly useful for problems requiring on-site response such as hardware problems at the customer site. You can explain these time limits to customers, so they can help set the proper priorities.

While you can set expectations for the response to a problem and the effort to resolve it, you can't determine the actual time-to-resolution in advance. No one knows how difficult or time consuming any one problem will be.

Hold the number of problems assigned a high priority to a practical minimum, since your Help Desk can only work on a given number of many problems at once. Typically, the Help Desk manager needs to approve a high priority designation.

One technique for evaluating your Help Desk could be determining whether your Help Desk uses high priorities too often; this indicates an over-reaction to the severity of problems.

Call ownership

When you escalate a call to another area, who is responsible for resolving the problem? Most organizations prefer to keep the ownership at the Help Desk. This provides one contact point for the customer, consistency in determining if a problem is really solved, and one collection point for unresolved problems. It also reinforces customers who call the Help Desk for support, and discourages them from calling multiple areas.

Call follow-up

It may not be possible for your Help Desk to followup every problem it handles to ensure the customer is satisfied. When considering which problems to follow up, consider the following points.

Priority-one problems should come first; always follow up these to be sure the problem was solved.

If customers are irritated, you may not feel like talking with them again. However, it is important to follow up. Customers will probably be surprised to hear back from the Help Desk and may be more pleasant in the future.

Followup with repeat callers to be sure they didn't call back simply out of frustration. This follow-up enhances the perception of the Help Desk and makes these customer more likely to call in the future.

Any problem assigned to another area is also a likely candidate for a follow-up call. The assignee should deal with the Help Desk to close the problem, but the customer should have the opportunity to agree the problem has been resolved.

Also follow up problems you resolved on first contact that had a high dollar impact or affected a large number of customers.

If the customer does not agree that the problem has been resolved, then you may need to reopen the problem record, document the customer's current experience of the problem, and make another attempt to resolve the problem.

chapter **8**

Problem assignment and resolution

Your Help Desk should strive to solve as many calls on first contact as possible. In cases where you don't have the resources to solve the problem, your Help Desk needs to assign the problem to another area. The organization or individual receiving the assignment is called the assignee. Be sure to keep some measurements on the percentage of calls received that you need to assign; a high number may indicate insufficient Help Desk training.

We'll be using three key terms throughout this chapter: assignment, escalation, and notification. You may find that Help Desks define these terms differently or use them interchangeably. However, your organization needs to use these terms consistently throughout your Help Desk operations. We've defined these terms in the following paragraphs.

Assignment   This process involves passing lead resolution responsibility from the Help Desk to another organization or individual predetermined by procedures to handle that type of problem.

Escalation   In the escalation process, Help Desk agents or managers notify senior staff members (often of several different organizations), so they are aware of the situation and can apply appropriate resources to resolve the problem.

Notification   This process involves communicating the nature and severity of the problem to customer representatives, so they may take steps to mitigate the impact to their organizations.

In the pages that follow, we'll discuss the assignment, escalation, and notification processes in detail, so you can implement these processes at your Help Desk to more quickly and accurately resolve your customers' problems.

Assignment process

Problem assignment at the Help Desk is generally made by routing the call to another organization based on documented procedures. These procedures identify support coverage based upon the type of problem, time of day, day of week, problem priority, and escalation status.

Your Help Desk needs to have an understanding with the management and staff of the assignee area that they will handle problems according to the priority of the problem and the organization's service level commitments.

Even when you assign a problem, the Help Desk continues to own it from the customer's point of view.

The Help Desk must track the progress of the organization that is now driving the problem resolution.

Determining severity codes

Escalate problems to management based on the initial severity and after a specified period passes. The problem severity code and application area determine how and to whom the problem is escalated. Some firms use a problem coordinator or network availability manager to establish severity codes. Others route problems by classification code to the head of the specific problem area and establish the severity codes at that level. Although in the past the Help Desk typically set the severity code when a problem was reported, more firms now work with customers in advance to define severity codes based on well-defined problem types and customer impacts.

Managing the data

The data your Help Desk supplies to an assignee depends on the system you use. Generally, the assignee should have the information initially reported to the Help Desk. You should also communicate the priority level to the assignee.

Direct contact between the assignee and the customer should be the exception rather than the rule. Over time, such contact may result in the customer directly calling these technical support personnel. At many Help Desks, agents call the customers and conference in the assignee. This also helps keep the Help Desk current on problem status. In some cases, assignees may need to contact the caller directly, but they should not leave a name or telephone number.

How to provide data to the assignee

Your Help Desk may use an automated problem handling system as the primary source for providing problem information to the assignee. The problem report is routed on the system and can be accessed by the assignee as well as Help Desk personnel. The system can supply a date/time stamp to document when a problem is opened. For priority problems, the Help Desk will likely call assignees to be sure they receive the information and clearly understand the facts and severity.

Some organizations use call log sheets or trouble tickets to communicate problem assignment information. Such forms also generally allow the assignee to document the resolution.

Your Help Desk should establish procedures to ensure the person receiving the problem is provided with all necessary information. One method is to meet with each department and determine what information is critical in resolving problems related to its area. The Help Desk uses this information to customize or create sub-screens on the problem management system to capture the needed information for specific problem types.

Some companies use display bulletin boards to alert the Help Desk staff of current outstanding problems. This is necessary to prevent multiple assignments. When the Help Desk receives a call for an already reported problem, agents can reference the previous problem and add new information to the log. This way, agents don't assign the problem or manage it as new.

Data elements to track

Help Desks maintain numerous tools and techniques to record, assign, resolve, track, report, and manage problems. Help Desks use this data to analyze problem

1. Problem number
2. Problem type/ subtype
3. Component
4. Workstation
5. Node
6. Transactions
7. Error code
8. Application
9. Job number
10. Step number
11. Program name
12. Region
13. Network address
14. Serial number
15. Product
16. Problem symptom
17. Problem classification
18. Problem category
19. Cause code
20. Problem priority
21. Reported by/ reported to
22. Location
23. Phone number
24. Assigned to (multiple)
25. Time/date fields
    Reported
    Occurred
    Assigned (multiple)
    Assignee received (multiple)
    Vendor called
    Vendor opened
    Vendor closed
    Resolved (multiple)
    Closed
26. Actions taken
27. Narrative ("search on" text)
28. Frequency of occurrence
29. Reference to other related problems

Figure 8-1   Elements you can use when tracking problems

histories, monitor open problems, create reports, support meetings, and monitor vendors.

Figure 8-1 presents a sample list of data elements Help Desks track. Agents gather much of this information during problem recording.

Although several organizations maintain problem histories from "day one," companies with integrated problem history information typically limit the amount of on-line problem history to enhance response time. An average duration for maintaining on-line problem history is six to 12 months; after that, the Help Desk archives the data to off-line files. For long-term tracking, agents can later process this data in batch mode or temporarily restore it to on-line storage.

Be sure to consider security concerns such as who should be allowed to view, input, or update problem tracking data elements. This is especially true for authorization to close problems and for archiving or deleting data.

Assignment techniques

Assignment techniques usually depend on the problem classification codes and problem severity. Many Help Desks have a list of first, second, and third persons to contact for a specific category. The reference list may include office phone numbers, E-mail addresses, home phones, pager numbers, and car phone numbers. You can automate this reference assignment list or print it on hard copy. Keeping the list up to date, and maintaining easy access to this list is vital.

Assignment techniques vary by organization and priority of the problem. A few assignment techniques include using primary and backup support staff, holding daily meetings, escalating unsolved problems, and conducting management reviews.

	Initial priority level	Time unresolved	Escalated to priority level
Problem #1	2	one day	1
Problem #2	3	three days	2

Figure 8-2   Sample priority escalation procedure

Primary and backup support staff   Many companies use a cross-reference list to assign problems to support groups during regular business hours. The list is kept on-line by application and is often supplemented by a daily on-call list. After hours, companies may supply on-call staff with pagers, and list these staff members by individual or by application.

Daily meetings   Assignment procedures typically include daily morning meetings. The Help Desk manager reviews open problems with the staff and other managers and ensures all responsible parties receive the information they need to resolve the problems. Help Desks can also assign problems by conference calls or teleconference. For example, the Help Desk of a large financial concern manages open problems with remote sites by conducting daily video conferences.

Escalating unsolved problems   The relationship of assigned problems to escalation varies from organization to organization. Figure 8-2 presents an example of a priority escalation procedure.

Usually, assignment to a second-level support group does not require escalation. If a problem requires assignment to third-level support, or if a problem has remained unsolved beyond a specified period – perhaps a full day – then the Help Desk will escalate that problem. The degree of escalation is based on the problem's effect on the company's ability to do business as well as the length of time since the problem occurred.

Some organizations escalate open problems first to the Help Desk manager and, later, involve upper-level staff and executive managers if the problem continues. The number of escalations that occur until the problem reaches top management depends on the type of problem. No matter how many people become involved, the Help Desk must stay aware of all escalated problems and get regular updates on its current status. This is critical for the Help Desk's credibility and the manager's credibility.

Escalating the priority of a problem is ordinarily a management decision. It may involve a higher level of management depending on the severity level or the number of times the Help Desk has had to escalate the problem.

Management review   At higher levels of management, such as vice presidents, problem escalation is informational in nature. This is often called notification, since these managers usually aren't able to resolve problems but may need to know their status. A strictly followed escalation and notification policy, with no informal hand-offs, is critical to problem management.

Importance of Help Desk ownership

Never tell customers to call another area for problem resolution. This can result in a host of problems for both the Help Desk and customers.

If customers call other areas for support, it may negatively affect the productivity of the customers and the assigned area. Customers may not be able to reach anyone in that area, or they may have misstated the symptoms of the problem – or the Help Desk may have misinterpreted the symptoms – and the problem may require a different assignee.

In addition, if another area resolves a problem, information valuable to the solution may be lost. For example, other Help Desk callers may be experiencing the same problem, so the assignee would be receiving unnecessary calls.

When customers go directly to other areas for support, the Help Desk may not know if or when the problem is resolved, and customers could end up getting the runaround.

Customer notification

When major systems or applications problems occur, the Help Desk can play a crucial role in minimizing the impact on its customers, even though it is usually beyond the ability of the Help Desk to resolve those problems directly.

Customer notification involves informing the customer community of major systems problem, so customers know the Help Desk and appropriate support groups are aware of the problem and will provide updates on the resolution status.

Note that we distinguish notification from escalation. The people we notify – our customers – have a need to be aware of a problem but are not necessarily expected to have a role in resolving it.

Purpose of notification

Customer notification can have a major, positive impact on customer productivity and satisfaction, because it alerts customers to problems and keeps them informed. Notification can also positively impact the Help Desk's productivity – it prevents repeat phone calls and interruptions, allowing agents to concentrate on the problem at hand.

Using various techniques, the Help Desk can notify the impacted customer groups of information such as the expected duration of an outage, status updates, and outage recovery.

Customer notification contributes to customer productivity and satisfaction by letting customers know a problem is a general problem not associated with their individual terminals. It prevents downtime when agents can instruct customers on ways to work around the problem. Notification also gets customers back to work as quickly as possible once the outage problem is resolved and makes it clear to the customer community that the Help Desk is aware of the importance of their work.

Notification techniques

Many Help Desks create matrices indicating the segments of a customer population that are impacted by the failure of particular applications, particular systems, or even single hardware components. This enables the Help Desk to provide specific information and helps agents communicate the severity of a problem to the appropriate support groups.

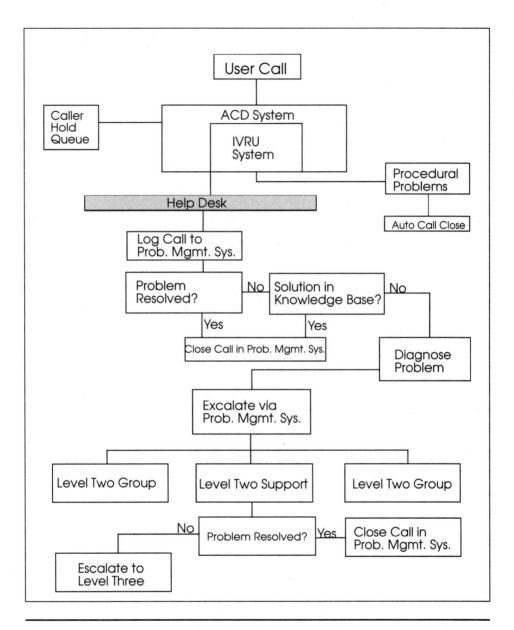

Figure 8-3 **Flow chart showing problem resolution at a typical Help Desk**

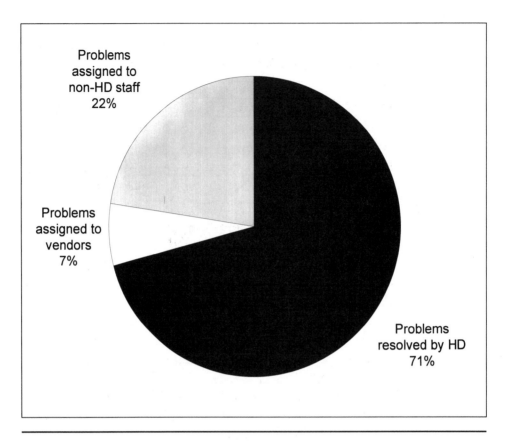

Figure 8-4 **Chart from Help Desk Institute's 1993 *Help Desk Practices Survey* showing the percentage of problems solved by the Help Desk**

Telephone messages Use system-wide voice mail or call customer centers or departments and give the message to a point person.

Digital recorders Place notification message on an auto attendant, so incoming callers hear the message before they reach an agent. In many instances, this is all they need to know and they hang up.

Electronic display boards   These can be helpful and cost effective for large customer sites or in critical areas such as senior management headquarters or central data centers.

Electronic mail   This tool is helpful for notifying all your customers or providing specific information to specific customers.

Pagers   Help Desks usually only use pagers to notify senior managers of problems rather than customers.

Problem resolution

Resolution is achieving a satisfactory result for the customer without assigning the call to another department.

Depending upon the nature of the calls, the staff resources available, and the systems and information in use, Help Desks can resolve between 20 to 98% of calls. Many mature Help Desks consistently resolve 80 to 90% of incoming calls. In fact, knowledgeable agents can resolve many problems during the initial call based on the information they receive and their experience.

Figure 8-3 illustrates the problem resolution process at a typical Help Desk. Figure 8-4 shows the percentage of resolved problems at the average Help Desk, according to Help Desk Institute's 1993 *Survey of Help Desk Practices*.

Access to problem history and configuration data enhances the Help Desk's ability to resolve problems when receiving calls. Searching problem history in an automated system using problem types and key words can help you resolve problems. Formalized shift turnover procedures also help gather and disburse recent resolution information as well as information on outstanding problems.

When you can't resolve problems during the initial call, offer customers several suggestions for working around the problem and give them an estimate of the time it might take to resolve the problem and call them back.

When you need specialists' help to resolve problems and they are not immediately available, customers often must wait for a return call. Therefore, you need to record the details of the problem for the person assigned to the situation. Recording this information reduces the details the customer will need to repeat to the specialist.

Closing problems

Does your Help Desk resolve and close problems without adequately documenting the cause? Many organizations address this issue by making problem resolution and problem closing separate steps.

In many Help Desks, the agent who resolves the problem is not the same person who closes the problem. For escalated problems, the assignee – the person who resolves the problem – should not be the person who closes the problem in the system. The Help Desk should follow up and close the problem with the customer's approval. Closing problems separately from resolution of problems ensures only Help Desk staff can record the problem's cause and its resolution.

chapter **9**

Tracking and reporting trends

Of all the functional areas within an IS organization, the Help Desk is best equipped to develop problem trend reports for measuring and reporting problem resolution and vendor performance. By using reports, graphs, and meetings, the Help Desk can focus management's attention on the priority issues affecting the customer community. The goal is to ask, "why do we have this problem trend?" and, "what can we do to eliminate it?"

In this chapter, we'll discuss how to establish an effective reporting method and realize the benefits of problem analysis.

1. Lost customer productivity
2. Time consumed by Help Desk staff
3. Computer reruns
4. Difficult or clumsy system designs
5. Hardware, communication lines, or modems that frequently fail
6. Vendors who provide poor response and service
7. Internal assignees who do not resolve problems quickly enough to meet service level commitments
8. Lost time by customers unable to contact Help Desk personnel on the first call
9. Higher than necessary phone bills to respond to recurring problems
10. High shipping costs to deliver rerun computer reports or deliver parts for broken hardware
11. Lost customer revenue

Figure 9-1   Organizational information Help Desks can track

Track the trends

Help Desks must commit resources to accurately track and monitor problem trends. Usually, organizations need to commit separate resources for analyzing and interpreting problems, so the Help Desk can continue providing effective real-time responses. Without problem analysis and interpretation, the Help Desk doesn't focus on how to eliminate recurring problems and best serve the customer community.

Help Desks need to take responsibility for problem analysis. It's easy to let the daily tasks of taking calls and monitoring problem resolution consume your Help Desk. Under such conditions, the Help Desk conducts little problem analysis. Often, the problem analysis that Help Desks do conduct involves simply developing reports requested by senior managers. For this reason, Help Desk managers need to allocate sufficient resources for problem analysis and shelter these people – as much as possible – from the day-to-day crises of the Help Desk's.

Because of their roles at the Help Desk, agents and managers have more direct exposure to customers' problems and concerns than any other employees within an organization. Figure 9-1 presents some of the problems, trends, and concerns the Help Desk can help track and report. This information can be invaluable to the entire organization.

How to establish an effective reporting method

Effective reporting begins by tracking easily measured statistics. These statistics include total number of calls opened, closed, and outstanding; calls by problem type; average response time; and network availability.

Your Help Desk can begin by tracking an area you can easily measure on a monthly basis, then documenting ideas to improve the area. This sets a successful precedent, reduces the fear of tracking statistics, and paves the way for more specific reporting such as by individual staff member and by application areas.

The next step in reporting involves clearly presenting the information. You can improve problem analysis by showing percentages by categories including total calls by problem type, unit (such as application), and

Frequency	Report description	Purpose or use
Daily	Problems recorded by or assigned to staff members – grouped by department	Provided to department managers for human resource management
Daily	All open problems and recent problem resolutions by problem type, customer, and assignee	Used to support Help Desk and data center meetings
Weekly	Total calls, totals by type of call (such as hardware or software) and response times	Transmitted electronically to customers in memo form with tips and techniques based on problem trends
Monthly	Calls by application including problem response time and one line of description for open problems	Provided to managers of application areas
Monthly	Calls by problem type on an hourly, daily, and weekly basis	Used by the Help Desk to analyze problem trends in on-line, off-line, and network availability
Monthly	Call volume by type and device as well as hardware downtime	Provided to managers for service level comparisons

Figure 9-2   **Problem analysis and tracking reports**

Frequency	Report description	Purpose or use
Monthly	Graphs of calls by priority level including resolution rates and problem types	Used by the Help Desk to analyze problem trends
Monthly	Calls by assignee, customer group or organization, device type, item type, key item affected, problem type, and cause type	Provided to upper management to determine training and programming needs
Monthly	Availability by region, application, network, and controller	Provided to managers for service level comparisons
Monthly	Graphs and bar charts showing terminal and modem failures and chronic problems	Provided to vendors in evaluating products and services
Monthly	Pie charts showing total call volume by problem type	Provided to managers for meeting support

Figure 9-2   Problem analysis and tracking reports (continued)

customer or department. Use these percentages to produce memos, graphs, pie charts, and other easy-to-read documents. Keep in mind that you want to provide quick, concise overviews.

Help Desks can create graphic reports automatically from a problem management system or manually by entering data into PC-based graphics systems or other presentation tools that allow file transfer of the data.

You can enhance reports and other forms of analysis by including major data center events, changes, and improvements within the reporting period. Using this method, you can easily communicate recommendations for future improvements, and you can estimate how upcoming events will impact Help Desk management and staffing purposes.

Figure 9-2 shows the variety of daily, weekly, and monthly problem analysis and tracking reports Help Desks use and presents some of the ways Help Desks use these reports.

Once your Help Desk establishes a problem reporting and analysis precedent, you can contact managers for each area to learn what other information would be beneficial. You can then develop additional reports such as tracking problems by type to analyze the performance of applications, departments, and hardware.

Benefits of problem analysis

Reducing the need for calls is a primary long-term goal of Help Desk analysis; however, the ultimate result is to improve bottom-line costs. One way to illustrate bottom-line results is to measure the cost of human time, out-of-pocket expenses associated with the most significant problems, and the related lost revenues (or value of lost opportunities). You can do this during slow periods with assistance from accounting personnel. You can then graph problem costs and rank problems by the financial impact on the organization. These figures could help you allocate additional resources to problem resolution and Help Desk activities.

Organizations offering automated systems and support as their primary business often use estimates of problem costs to focus management's attention on situations the company can eliminate or reduce the frequency of occurrence.

The reports and charts the Help Desk generates also help companies identify intermittent problems and less evident problems. The Help Desk can also track and communicate chronic problems, such as repetitive troubles with terminals and modems, by evaluating vendor and product performance.

Your Help Desk can then use the information in these reports to recommend and purchase standard products and negotiate maintenance agreements. Many companies use problem reports to recommend educational and programming measures, research specific complaints, and evaluate vendor responsiveness. Additionally, you can provide these statistics to the customer base along with hints and techniques that address and prevent common or repetitive problems.

chapter 10

Expert systems

Expert systems are a subset of a broad field of computer development called artificial intelligence. Other activities in this field include imaging, voice processing, and game simulation. The term *expert systems* generally refers to complex computer systems that deduce – or infer – information based on matching actual events against a predefined set of rules or knowledge. In Help Desk applications, expert systems narrow down the type of problem and suggest probable and possible resolutions.

Expert systems can save you time, help solve your customers' problems, and make your Help Desk more efficient. In fact, some developers promote expert systems as the premier solution to Help Desks' automation problems. However, plunging headlong into such a system without thorough research and careful planning could cost your organization huge amounts of time and money and may not yield the desired benefits.

Most expert system shells on the market for Help Desks fall into three categories: rules-based, case-based, and decision-tree. We'll discuss these systems in this chapter and present additional information to help you determine how and when to use an expert system at your Help Desk.

Rules-based systems

Rules-based systems – often called expert or knowledge-based – use rules known as heuristics. These rules focus on key aspects of a particular problem or application and manipulate a set of logic rules to reason through the knowledge they are given. For those familiar with computer programming, these rules generally fall into the "if – then, else" type of logic.

The systems "think" by using the rules joined through a method called chaining – the technique for linking knowledge. These links can run forward or backward. Forward chaining is a method of reasoning in which the program reasons toward a goal. It seeks to identify all rules whose "if" portions are true and uses the "then" portions of those rules to find other rules that are also true. Backward chaining is the most common. In this system, the program forms a hypothesis and works backward to prove it, seeking the rules whose "then" portions match the "if" portions.

The portion of the system containing the control strategies and the process the system uses to derive new facts from known facts is called the inference engine.

Rules-based systems were built first and offer several advantages: many systems are available, they can be precise, the logic rules are easy to follow, and they work well for a narrow scope of knowledge that is relatively stable.

However, the disadvantages may outweigh the advantages: The logic strings tend to be long and complex, and they require a significant amount of pre-programming and maintenance by an "expert" to work well. Plus, it can be challenging to keep the rules up-to-date in a rapidly changing environment.

Case-based systems

Case-based systems follow a different type of logic to match real-life events against their knowledge databases. The inference engine in a case-based system isolates key components of a problem and searches for existing cases on the database with the highest percentage match against those key components.

For example, let's say a customer can't get a report to print on a network laser printer and calls your Help Desk. Using a case-based system, you would key in variables such as customer identification, location of the printer, and network information. The inference engine will search for past cases or instances that contain those variables on its database. The system might find three cases in descending order of "hit rate" against those variables and suggest further questions to check against other variables.

The advantages of case-based systems are that the "match" method of thinking more closely emulates the way an expert thinks, it takes less time to identify a likely solution with the customer on the phone, and these systems can "learn" new solutions as you add more solved problems to the problem database – reducing the level of expertise required to set up the system and making the system easier to maintain.

On the other hand, case-based systems tend to be expensive and may not be right for you if you're setting up a new Help Desk with no problem histories to load into the system.

Decision-tree systems

The third major type of technology used for expert systems is called a decision-tree. This is the simplest type of expert system. Essentially, a decision-tree uses a branching approach to store and retrieve knowledge. And it generally provides a graphical, tree-style interface you use to find information.

Simply put, a decision-tree provides a series of two branching options. Often, these options are presented in the form of yes or no questions. Depending on your answer, the decision-tree branches one way or another. In contrast, a rules-based expert system can use a complex series of rules to arrive at information. In addition, rules-based systems generally don't provide a graphical interface.

The primary benefit of decision-tree systems is that they are easy to set up. In addition, a decision-tree makes it relatively easy to add new knowledge, and they are easy to use to retrieve knowledge. However, decision-tree expert systems aren't adequate for complex knowledge systems.

When to use expert systems

It's easy to spend a great deal of time and money on expert systems with varying degrees of success – unless you've carefully researched systems and chosen the one that's right for your Help Desk. Below, we've presented some issues to consider when evaluating expert systems.

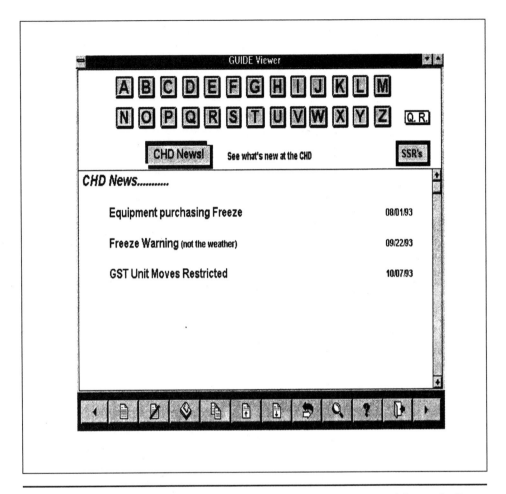

Figure 10-1   An opening screen from Owl Industries' "Guide," an expert system (courtesy of IDS)

Priorities   Evaluate your Help Desk's need for an expert system against all the Help Desk's automation opportunities. Many Help Desks have tremendous productivity enhancements available through call-handling automation and customer database development. These projects tend to offer high paybacks with low risk. Consider purchasing an expert system after you have implemented other, simpler automation steps

1st CLASS, 1st Class Expert Systems, Inc., Wayland, MA

Aion Development System (ADS), Aion Corporation, Palo Alto, CA

Apriori, Answer Computer, Inc., Sunnyvale, CA

Computer-Aided Intelligent Service (CAIS) Expert Diagnostic Module, Rosh Intelligent Systems Inc., Needham, MA

CBR Express, Inference Corporation, Los Angeles, CA

Crystal, Intelligent Environments, Boston, MA

Expert Advisor, Software Artistry, Inc., Indianapolis, IN

Expert Systems Development and Training, Oxko Corp., Annapolis, MD

Goldworks II, Gold Hill Computer, Inc., Cambridge, MA

HelpDesk Expert Automation Tool (HEAT), Bendata Management Systems, Inc., Colorado Springs, CO

KEE, Intellicorp, Inc., Mountain View, CA

Knowledge Engineering System, Software Architecture and Engineering, Inc. Arlington, VA

Knowledgepro, Knowledge Garden, Inc., Nassau, NY

Level 5, Information Builders, Inc., New York, NY

Nexpert Object, Neuron Data, Palo Alto, CA

Personal Consultant Easy, Texas Instruments, Houston, TX

Professional Help Desk Adviser, Legent Corp, Vienna, VA

Remind: A case-based reasoning development shell, Cognitive Systems, Inc., Boston, MA

Figure 10-2   Expert systems tools and developers

Artificial Intelligence 3rd Edition, by Patrick Winston, published by Addison Wesley, 1992

Expert Systems: Artificial Intelligence in Business, by Paul Harmon and David King, published by John Wiley & Sons, Inc., New York, 1985

Expert Systems: Tools and Applications, by Paul Harmon, published by John Wiley & Sons, Inc., New York, 1990

Off to Seize the Wizard: The Revolution in Service Automation, by Jeff Pepper, published by ServiceWare Inc., 1993

The Rise of the Expert Company, by Edward Feigenbaum, H. Penny Nii and Pamela McCorduck, published by Time Books, 1988

Figure 10-3   Reference material on expert systems

or as part of a preplanned sequence of events in an overall automation strategy.

Types of problems   In most expert systems implementations, the key to success rests with the ability to keep the knowledge database complete, accurate, and current. This is easiest if your Help Desk deals with a narrow scope of problems. Or perhaps 80% of the calls your Help Desk receives reflects 10 general problems. Be sure to track and understand your Help Desk's data when researching these systems.

Availability of expertise   Setting up and maintaining the knowledge database can be time consuming, particularly for rules-based systems. If an expert system is right for your Help Desk but your programming support is limited, consider implementing a case-based or decision-tree system. In addition, you'll want to encourage senior agents to continually update expert systems. This will capture and share their expertise with novice staff members, especially when senior agents transfer out of the Help Desk.

Target user   Trained agents can learn very complex problems quickly; in some instances, initially successful expert system installations have fallen by the wayside, because the staff became just as knowledgeable as the system – and faster. Therefore, one approach for implementing an expert system is to make it available to the customer. Figure 10-1 shows an opening screen from a customer-accessible expert system.

When customers use these systems directly, problem resolutions may not require an agent's time. Also, consider using an expert system as a training companion for new agents; this can help make them more productive while they are still learning.

Getting started

Figure 10-2 lists available expert systems tools and developers. And Figure 10-3 presents reference materials on the subject. Remember, when planning to implement an expert system for your Help Desk, be sure to thoroughly research these tools to determine the one that best suits your organization.

When purchasing expert system shells to create and personalize, you may need to commit additional resources to fund the development of your system. These resources may include purchasing adequate hardware to implement the system, hiring a consultant to personalize the system for your Help desk, and training your staff to efficiently use the system.

For rules-based systems, you may need programmers (or knowledge engineers) who can write using an expert system shell or language, human experts to provide the knowledge used to build the rules, and programmers to frequently update the rule logic.

chapter 11

Change management
and the Help Desk

Change management is the strategic system organizations use to manage and control the process of implementing changes in hardware, software, or communication links within a company. Help Desks use change management strategies to minimize the negative impact to their customers.

In this chapter, we'll discuss the importance of change management and how you can help drive this process at your Help Desk and your organization.

Smoothing the change process

Change management has gained increasing importance for Help Desks, because it impacts the levels of service Information Services provides. When a failure occurs within a company as a result of a change in hardware, software, or communications links, the Help Desk is often the first to know. With adequate involvement in the change management process, the Help Desk can isolate problems more readily, improve systems' availability by having changes backed out more quickly if problems develop, develop work-arounds in advance or on the spot, and help smooth the change process for customers.

The Help Desk's role in change management should be active and participatory. Your Help Desk should approve all changes before implementation. Before authorizing the change, review the change documentation as well as testing, back-out, and recovery procedures.

Your Help Desk should be able to access change status on-line and use automatic back-outs to remove changes that result in serious or chronic problems. You'll also want to ensure level-two and level-three support personnel are available at the time changes are implemented.

In addition, be sure customers and Help Desk personnel have received appropriate training before the change implementation, and work with the person making the change to assure continuous, quality service and customer satisfaction.

As a Help Desk agent, you may act as a customer liaison to the change committee by expressing concerns regarding the impact of proposed changes from the customers' points of view. For major, new implementations, ensure adequate information is available and support structures are in place to provide effective problem management.

Help desks can also play a larger role in application development and design as well as systems standardization. For example, you might make it standard for your company to provide on-line documentation for the Help Desk and customers before the company installs new hardware or software.

chapter **12**

Disaster recovery and the Help Desk

Disaster recovery planning becomes increasingly important as businesses become more dependent on their data processing operations.

Whether your company has a full-blown contingency center or limited procedures for disaster recovery, the Help Desk usually plays a key role in facilitating communications during this critical period. Therefore, in addition to supporting the company's overall plan, Help Desk managers should create disaster plans for their own centers. Your plan should be based on business cost/benefit justifications.

This chapter presents tips for creating a strategic disaster recovery plan for your Help Desk.

1. Procedures and systems for emergency communications following a disaster
2. Emergency staffing guidelines based on the geography of the local area and home locations of key employees
3. Emergency reconfiguration capabilities and procedures to allow partial restoration of data processing facilities.

Figure 12-1   Three components of a Help Desk disaster recovery plan

1. Notify technical support, discuss the problem, and anticipate outage time frames.

2. Notify customers on the incoming call queue using a recorded message or other tools such as scrolling screen displays and outgoing phone calls.

3. Post a sign in the Help Desk area to alert walk-up customers to the condition of the system.

4. Keep customers posted on the status of the condition and resolution.

Figure 12-2   Actions to include in a short-term disaster recovery plan

How to create
a disaster recovery plan

Figure 12-1 presents three components Help Desk managers usually include in disaster recovery plans. These components are procedures and systems for emergency communications following a disaster, emergency staffing guidelines based on the geography of the local area and home locations of key employees, and emergency reconfiguration capabilities and procedures to allow partial restoration of data processing facilities.

Some plans call for companies to set up contingency operations sites with a full complement of contingency hardware and telecommunications. These sites can be internal company data processing centers backing each other up, other companies' data processing centers supported by agreements to back up each others' operations, or facilities leased from companies that specialize in disaster recovery.

Some organizations establish complete disaster recovery plans, supplemented by short-term disaster recovery plans.

The Help Desk plays an important role in short-term disasters such as power outages. Figure 12-2 presents four actions you'll want to include in a short-term disaster recovery plan to communicate the status of the situation to technical support personnel and your customers. These actions could include notifying technical support, discussing the problem, and forming anticipated outage time frames; notifying customers on the incoming call queue using a recorded message or using other tools such as scrolling screen displays and outgoing phone calls; posting a sign in the Help Desk area to alert walk-up customers to the condition of the system; and keeping customers posted on the status of the condition and resolution.

Some organizations schedule disaster recovery drills; others periodically test portions of their disaster recovery plans. You'll need to weigh whether you should notify your staff of these drills. This is a trade-off between maximizing the spontaneous nature of the drill and minimizing the disruption it causes.

13

Service agreements and the Help Desk

Service agreements help you clarify expectations and set goals for the quality of service your Help Desk provides to your customers and the service you receive from service providers. This chapter presents guidelines for establishing service agreements with customers as well as with external and internal service providers.

Service agreements with customers

Providing your customers with an understanding of how to best use the Help Desk and what service expectations they should have is critical in operating a successful Help Desk. Service agreements help you

1. Help Desk hours

2. Response times associated with initial call handling

3. Average and maximum resolution times

4. Guidelines for problem resolution when various types of problems are assigned to internal or external

5. Customer responsibilities when reporting problems

6. Help Desk procedures for keeping customers informed on the status of open problems

7. Procedures for problem escalation

8. Software products supported

9. System availability

10. Network availability

11. Data integrity, security, and back-up

12. Scheduled jobs and delivery times

13. Charge backs or cost allocations

14. Educational support

Figure 13-1 **Fourteen points to consider when drawing up agreements with customer departments**

achieve these understandings. They are contracts between two organizations that establish mutual expectations and provide a standard to measure performance against.

Agreements with customer departments

You'll want to record any agreement between the Help Desk and one or more customer departments in your organization in a jointly developed document. This document should clearly state the level of service your Help Desk strives to provide, and it will help clarify your customers' expectations of your Help Desk.

Figure13-1 presents information to consider when drawing up agreements with customer departments. These agreements should include response times, average and maximum resolution times, procedures for problem assignment and escalation, software products supported, educational support, and charge backs or cost allocations.

Monitoring service levels

Monitoring your Help Desk's service levels – whether you have a formal agreement or not – is important, because monitoring provides information to make ongoing improvements in serving your customers.

Monitoring your Help Desk's service levels provides information on the actual service level your Help Desk provides, shows service improvements, and provides visibility for your Help Desk. Monitoring also helps you plan staffing changes or additions, helps show achievements and motivates your staff, and helps clarify your service relationship with your customers.

Actual service level provided   Once you establish service levels, you need to carefully measure your Help Desk's performance against these set targets. This verifies whether your Help Desk is achieving your defined service levels.

Service improvement   The primary reason for monitoring service is to ensure your Help Desk is meeting established targets. Once the Help Desk staff regularly achieves these targets, the next step is to redefine those targets and further improve levels of service. You can only improve service levels when you regularly measure them.

Service visibility   Regularly publishing detailed service data brings service to the attention of Help Desk personnel as well as Information Services management. The published figures bring focus to the Help Desk and provide an opportunity for you to present and discuss this information with IS and customer management.

Staffing plans   Monitoring service trends is invaluable when planning for staffing changes and justifying these changes to IS management.

Staff motivation   Staff members providing service often feel they are working hard without achieving any concrete or positive results. Establishing targets and monitoring service performance motivates agents to meet and exceed the targets. Monitoring gives the staff an incentive to work toward achieving the targets and also provides a clear identity for the Help Desk to management.

Clarify your service relationship with your customers   Service level agreements clarify the service your Help Desk will provide, and monitoring clearly shows your actual service against planned service levels.

Service agreements with service providers

Just as service agreements promote understanding with your customers, such contracts with your vendors and internal service partners promote understanding with your service providers. These agreements also help you measure the quality of services they provide.

Vendor service agreements

Service agreements with vendors can achieve a dramatic, measurable impact within your organization. Companies with established customer service agreements with maintenance vendors report savings of 5 to 40%. Some organizations justify their Help Desk budgets based on savings from such vendor maintenance agreements.

You should expect your hardware service vendors to provide high-quality, preventive maintenance to avoid as much unexpected downtime as possible. Once a problem occurs and vendors begin working toward a resolution, they should assume sufficient ownership. They should not place the problem back in the Help Desk's lap until they have resolved the problem. This helps minimize shifting the blame or denying responsibility when the problem is not corrected.

Remember, to resolve a problem, vendors must go through the same cycle – and require the same time – as your Help Desk. They require time to report, dispatch, diagnose, fix, and verify problems.

Many vendors now offer expanded services such as lists of known problems on electronic bulletin boards. Some vendors offer to become your "prime support" vendor – they will fix other manufacturers' products or help coordinate additional 'vendor services.

Monitoring service levels

Just as it's important for you to monitor Help Desk service levels on behalf of your customers, you need to monitor vendor service levels for your company. Since agreements are often tied to dollar incentives, these measurements can have a direct financial impact on your

Help Desk and can impact and clarify your Help Desk's relationship with vendors.

Escalating problems

Since contractual relationships with vendors are external, it's critical to escalate service problems promptly through the appropriate organization. In addition, the Help Desk often reports vendor responsibilities and performance to senior management; these reports help ensure your vendors actively work on timely, successful resolutions.

No other organization is better positioned to capture data on vendor performance than the Help Desk. For this reason, it's important to maintain consistent and accurate records of all aspects of vendor performance.

Agreements with internal service partners

Written service agreements with internal service partners – your assignees – are important, though the reason for having these may not be obvious to your service partners. These partners may be concerned that an attempt to document agreements represents unnecessary bureaucracy, or worse, a lack of trust.

From customers' perspectives and your perspective as the customer interface and representative, however, these agreements are just as important as vendor service agreements. The objective is to manage customers' expectations about service delivery during a problem. If the Help Desk doesn't have standards for time duration before an assignee takes a referred problem – or internal hardware service personnel arrive on site – then it will appear to the customer that the Help Desk agent is not managing the problem properly.

Internal service level agreements don't need to be lengthy or excessively detailed. The key is to include standards of performance during normal circumstances.

It's also important that Help Desk management doesn't use instances where standards aren't met as clubs to beat the service partner. Teamwork, as always, is critical.

chapter 14

Measuring the benefits of the Help Desk

Communicating the value of your Help Desk to IS and customer management in measurable terms is a multistep process. The first step is to justify the existence of your Help Desk. After that, the focus moves to your Help Desk's cost and service effectiveness.

In this chapter, we get down to nuts and bolts. We'll discuss how to measure the benefits your Help Desk provides to your customers, how to quantify Help Desk productivity, and how to measure the level of your customers' satisfaction. We've also included a sample Help Desk survey for you to review and adapt as you wish.

Justifying your Help Desk

The first step in communicating the value of your Help Desk is justifying its existence. A well-run Help Desk generates numerous benefits. One way to evaluate these benefits is to review your Help Desk's goals and objectives. Next, develop a means to determine whether your Help Desk meets these goals and objectives and, if so, the organizational impact. Measurement techniques might include measuring dollars saved by resolving problems quickly or eliminating the occurrence of certain problems. You can also monitor Help Desk productivity and conduct customer surveys to determine how well your Help Desk serves your customers.

Your company's accounting department can help you calculate the cost of direct labor including benefits and the cost of supervision. Use these figures to evaluate costs for the customer, the Help Desk, and assignee personnel. You can also include additional costs for reruns, delivery, vendor support, parts, supplies, phone calls, and other elements to determine problem costs. When your Help Desk reduces problems, it saves the organization these identifiable expenses.

One method to quantify cost savings is to sample your problem history, call the customers and others involved in the problem resolutions, and develop the typical costs for the most frequent and time-consuming problems. The Pareto Principle applies in this situation – the top 20% of your problems may represent 80% of your costs. Some of these costs may be easily identified, while you'll need to estimate other costs.

A graphical analysis should show Help Desk costs as well as costs incurred by customers, assignees, and related costs. A stacked line graph could show the cumulative cost of all factors, so you can project potential savings and cost avoidance if your Help Desk reduces the occurrence of certain problems in the future.

How to quantify Help Desk productivity

Measuring productivity is a vital component in measuring the success of your Help Desk. Productivity usually is the major focal point for management attention, second only to service. It provides a basis for justifying most Help Desk automation projects.

Help Desk managers usually have two sets of measurements they want to track: overall Help Desk productivity and individual Help Desk agent productivity.

Overall Help Desk productivity measures

The most obvious measures of overall Help Desk productivity are the numbers of problems the Help Desk handles and the percentage of problems resolved on first contact. This percentage varies depending on the type of problem calls received as well as the experience of the individuals and the resources available.

The percentage of problems resolved on first contact should increase as staff members proceed up the learning curve. Eventually, this percentage tends to level off, even for the most productive Help Desk agents. Another measure of productivity is how often Help Desk staff members escalate problems to the correct assignee, compared to the number of times problems must be reassigned.

Other productivity measures to consider include the number of devices supported per employee, calls handled per employee per month, and average hold times measured against calls per employee.

A less tangible measure of Help Desk productivity is the quality of recommendations made to reduce problem occurrences in the future. Use graphs to track the

1. Monitor performance according to stated service level commitments

2. Obtain ideas for improvement

3. Recognize agents' performances (both good and bad)

4. Identify trends

5. Improve customers' perceptions of the Help Desk by demonstrating an interest in customers' opinions

Figure 14-1   Five reasons to perform customer surveys

frequency of problems over time with notations about changes such as enhancements implemented at the suggestion of the Help Desk. Using this information, you can partially quantify the productivity gains you can credit to the Help Desk.

Individual staff productivity measures

Some individual productivity measures include calls handled per day, percentage of calls tallied or ticketed, percentage of problems requiring escalation, available time to take calls, and total minutes on the phone per day.

As a rule, productive agents have shorter conversations and handle a greater volume of calls. These agents should take care, however, not to offend customers by making them feel rushed. Also, plotting statistics on the number of calls handled per employee could be misleading, depending on the type of calls your Help Desk receives.

You'll want to monitor a wide variety of employee productivity measurements, but don't assess employees' performances directly from these measurements. Rather, use the information you gather as one input in an overall evaluation of how well the employee is doing. Customer service and satisfaction should always be the number one goal, and quality should rule over quantity. Misunderstanding these priorities can lead to disastrous results in both employee morale and customer satisfaction.

Customer surveys – measuring customer satisfaction

Another approach to assessing the impact of the Help Desk is to evaluate the customers' perceptions of services provided.

Why Help Desks conduct surveys

A Help Desk can look very good on paper by its own measurements of value and productivity, but to be successful, your Help Desk must enjoy the confidence and support of your customer base. The key is to be perceived as providing good service and quantify that perception. The best method for accomplishing this is direct feedback from the customer community – through customer surveys.

Figure 14-1 presents reasons your Help Desk should perform customer surveys. Such surveys help you monitor your Help Desk's performance according to stated service level commitments, obtain ideas for improvement, recognize agents' performances, identify trends, and improve customers' perceptions of the Help Desk by demonstrating an interest in their opinions.

Customer satisfaction survey

<tracking_#>

Part I – Help Desk service characteristics

The following list represents various characteristics of help desk service. In this section you are being asked to evaluate the <name_of_help_desk> at telephone number: <hd_tel_num>. We are using a five point scale, representing the range poor to excellent service, with a sixth option if the question or service is not applicable to the help desk. It should only take you about 10 minutes to fill out the entire survey, so please take your time and answer thoughtfully. Thank you for your assistance.

Characteristic of quality service	Your rating of the characteristic of service. Please circle the appropriate rating.	Comments you may wish to pass on to the help desk, especially if you give a below average rating.
	1 = Poor/Inadequate 2 = Fair (below average) 3 = Average (Meets needs) 4 = Good (Above average) 5 = Excellent/World Class	
Availability 1. Available, i.e. open for business when you need assistance.	1 2 3 4 5	

Figure 14-2   A sample Help Desk survey

Characteristic of quality service	Your rating of the characteristic of service. Please circle the appropriate rating.	Comments you may wish to pass on to the help desk, especially if you give a below average rating.
	1 = Poor/Inadequate 2 = Fair (below average) 3 = Average (Meets needs) 4 = Good (Above average) 5 = Excellent/World Class	

Access

2. Easy to reach by phone, E-mail, FAX, or other methods   1 2 3 4 5

3. Answering the phone in a reasonable period of time.   1 2 3 4 5

Responsiveness

4. Minimizing the amount of time you spend on hold.   1 2 3 4 5

5. Getting through to someone who can answer your questions.   1 2 3 4 5

Communications

6. Speaking clearly and using terms you understand.   1 2 3 4 5

7. Keeping you informed of progress toward an answer or solution.   1 2 3 4 5

Figure 14-2   A sample Help Desk survey (continued)

Characteristic of quality service	Your rating of the characteristic of service. Please circle the appropriate rating. ------------------------------------ 1 = Poor/Inadequate 2 = Fair (below average) 3 = Average (Meets needs) 4 = Good (Above average) 5 = Excellent/World Class	Comments you may wish to pass on to the help desk, especially if you give a below average rating.
Courtesy 8. Getting polite, friendly, people who are pleasant to deal with.	1 2 3 4 5	
Competence 9. Getting people with the appropriate skills, knowledge, and ability to help you.	1 2 3 4 5	
10. Taking time to completely understand your problem rather than just answer your question.	1 2 3 4 5	

Figure 14-2   A sample Help Desk survey continued

Characteristic of quality service	Your rating of the characteristic of service. Please circle the appropriate rating.	Comments you may wish to pass on to the help desk, especially if you give a below average rating.
	1 = Poor/Inadequate 2 = Fair (below average) 3 = Average (Meets needs) 4 = Good (Above average) 5 = Excellent/World Class	

Understanding the customer

11. Feeling that the Help Desk is interested in you and your problem.   1 2 3 4 5

12. Sensitivity to the urgency of your question or problem   1 2 3 4 5

Effectiveness

13. Getting solutions/ answers to your questions in a timely manner.   1 2 3 4 5

14. Pursuing hard to solve or complex issues.   1 2 3 4 5

Overall satisfaction

15. Overall level of support provided by the desk support.   1 2 3 4 5

Figure 14-2   A sample Help Desk survey (continued)

Customer satisfaction survey

<tracking_#>

Part II - Customer characteristics

These questions provide the necessary background information to help understand the trends and differences between surveys. Please answer all the questions according to the instructions for each question.

1.What type of work do you do that is supported by the Help Desk? (circle one):

a. Office/Clerical

b. Management/Professional (Doctor, Lawyer, Teacher, Manager, etc.)

c. Data Processing

d. Manufacturing/Assembly

e. Engineering

f. Other _____

2.How do you rate your experience and knowledge of the products or services supported by the Help Desk? (circle one):

a. No experience

b. Novice (low level)

c. Intermediate(moderate level)

d. Advanced knowledge(high level)

e. Expert

3.How often do you use the Help Desk? (circle one):

a. Never

b. Less than once a month

c. Once a month

d. More than once a month

e. Once a week

f. More than once a week

g. Daily

Figure 14-2   A sample Help Desk survey (continued)

4.How do you use the Help Desk? (circle all that apply):

a.   For product or process usage questions

b.   For training on the product or service

c.   To report product or service problems/defects

d.   To report hardware or network failures or outages

e.   For scheduling or purchasing products or services

f.   For an interface to my vendor

g.   As a substitute for reading the manual

h.   For someone to talk to when I am lonely

5.How much time would you estimate the Help Desk saves you each week? (circle one):

a.   None

b.   About 15 minutes

c.   About 30 minutes

d.   About 1 hour

e.   About 2 hours

f.   More than 2 hours but less than 4 hours

g.   Between 4 and 8 hours

h.   More than 8 hours

6.How often do you use resources other than this Help Desk for assistance? (circle one) Skip this question if you answered "never" to question 3:

a.   Never

b.   Up to 25% of the time

c.   Between 26 and 50% of the time

d.   Between 51% and 75% of the time

e.   More than 75% of the time

f.   Always

If you answered Never (f) to this question please skip the next question. You are finished.

Figure 14-2   A sample Help Desk survey (continued)

7.If you use other sources for assistance, who or what do you use for help?

(Please fill in the percentage of times you use each of the following sources so it totals 100%):

a. _____Other Help Desks or help lines within the company

b. _____Other outside Help Desks such as a vendors

c. _____Other people in your department

d. _____Friends in other departments or locations within the company

e. _____Friends outside of the company

f. _____Printed literature or manuals

g. _____Other (please specify the source)

Figure 14-2   A sample Help Desk survey (continued)

Developing useful surveys

When developing a survey for your Help Desk, consider the following points.

Determine the segments of your company or organization to survey. Should you give questionnaires to everyone in your company? Only to those customers the Help Desk has directly served? Or to a mix of customers and non-customers?

Decide how often you should ask for your customers' opinions: once a year, quarterly, monthly, or randomly. You can also link surveys to a service event or a fixed number of calls.

Determine how to give the survey to your customers. You can use company mail or E-mail, ask questions over the phone, or distribute surveys with an IS or Help Desk newsletter.

Carefully decide on the questions you ask and how to best phrase each question. Refer to Figure 14-2 for a sample survey.

Be sure to include an explanation about the purpose of your survey and how your customers, the Help Desk, and the company will benefit from the feedback these customers provide.

Make the survey short enough to prevent resistance to completing it. Indicate how, when, and where customers should return their surveys. Also, indicate a place for the customer's name and location, but mark this information as optional.

Don't have the same customers complete surveys too frequently; if you continually ask them to answer the same or similar questions, they won't be very enthusiastic about completing and returning the questionnaire.

Finally, provide survey results and a brief list of actions your Help Desk will take to those who participate in the survey.

Publishing results for management, Help Desk employees, and your customers

For continued feedback from the customer community, conduct and publish surveys every quarter. This allows you to plot trends and reduces the number of individuals your Help Desk surveys to a manageable quantity.

chapter 15

A final word

As corporations compete in the global economy, organizations' managements focus on reducing expenses while maintaining or improving customer service and market share.

Within Information Services, no organization is better placed to contribute to this goal than the Help Desk. The Help Desk provides focus to the problem management effort by giving the customer a single number to call for problem resolution. Additionally, it allows other IS functions to be more effective by relieving them of direct customer interface responsibilities.

Corporate senior management knows the value of your Help Desk. Don't let the constant complaints and crises inherent in the job discourage you. You and your team are at the heart of the action. Few jobs provide as much visibility and opportunities as team member and management positions at the Help Desk.

Remember, keep your Help Desk's purpose and objectives in mind, have a positive attitude, and understand your customers' needs as you work to resolve their problems and help your company meet its goals.

Index

A

ACD 72, 74, 75, 76, 78, 80, 81, 86
ACS 73
Auto attendant 72, 76, 77, 80, 82
Automatic call distribution 32
Automatic call distributor 74
Automatic call sequencer 72, 73
Automation 31, 78, 125, 129, 130, 131, 153

B

Burnout 51, 52, 53, 54

C

Call logging 88
Call routing table 80
Case-based systems 127, 128
Change management 17, 32, 33, 98, 136
Consolidation 17, 94
Customer community 14, 16, 23, 34, 41, 44, 45, 61, 88, 111, 112, 117, 118, 155, 163
Customer interface 19, 148, 165
Customer relations 43, 61, 62, 64, 67, 70
Customer satisfaction 32, 33, 136, 155

D

Data elements 106, 108
Decentralization 13, 17, 34
Decision-tree systems 128
Disaster recovery 139, 141, 142

E

Electronic mail 21, 68, 72, 83, 115
Electronic status display 26, 27
Escalate 103, 104, 105, 108, 109, 110, 112, 116, 144, 145, 148, 153, 154

Help
Desk
Institute.

Training, educational materials and a
networking forum for Help Desk professionals.

IT'S EASY TO ORDER

Quantity Discounts

10% discount when ordering 10 to 25 books of the same title. Need more than 25 of any one title? Please call for information about discounts.

Questions? Call:

From the US and Canada, call 800-248-5667. Worldwide, call 719-531-5138.

How to order:

Mail or FAX 719-528-4250 the completed order fom, indicating payment method to:
Help Desk Institute
1755 Telstar Drive
Suite 101
Colorado Springs, CO
80920-1017

Help Desk Institute Bookstore Order Form

ITEM	Member Price	Non-Member Price	Qty.	Cost
Help Desk U© 101 Kit Customer Service Skills for Help Desk Professionals	$995.00	$1095.00		
HDU 101 Additional Learner's Workbooks	39.95	49.95		
HDU 101 Additional videos	99.95	99.95		
Help Desk U© 102 Kit Successful Problem Solving Techniques for Help Desk Professionals	995.00	1095.00		
HDU 102 Additional Learner's Workbooks	39.95	49.95		
HDU 102 Additional videos	99.95	99.95		
Help Desk U© 201 Kit How to Manage and Improve Help Desk Operations	995.00	1095.00		
HDU 201 Additional Learner's Workbooks	39.95	49.95		
HDU 201 Additional videos	99.95	99.95		
HDI Video Seminar with Malcolm Fry: Set of 6 tapes	795.00	895.00		
The Help Desk Handbook	49.95	150.00		
LifeRaft Newsletter, one-year	36.00	96.00		
1993 Help Desk Buyers Guide	50.00	95.00		
1993 Help Desk Practices Survey	25.00	150.00		
1993 Help Desk Salary Survey	25.00	150.00		

More selections on following pages ...

METHOD OF PAYMENT

- ❑ **Please Invoice my company**
- ❑ **Check enclosed**
- ❑ **Visa** ❑ **Mastercard**
- ❑ **American Express**

Card # / P.O. #:

_____

Expiration Date:

_____

Signature:

_____

OUR GUARANTEE!

Should any book or gift item not meet your requirements, you will receive a full refund by returning it in reusable condition within 30 days of purchase.

HDI Focus Book: Customer Service Skills for Technical Support Professionals	6.95	9.95	
HDI Focus Book: Stress Management for Customer Support Professionals	6.95	9.95	
HDI Focus Book: Marketing the Help Desk to Senior Managers and Customers	6.95	9.95	
HDI Focus Book: Motivating and Managing Help Desk Professionals	6.95	9.95	
HDI Focus Book: How to Select and Use Outsource Services for your Hlep Desk	6.95	9.95	
HDI Focus Book: How to Measure Customer Satisfaction	6.95	9.95	
Tips on Evaluating and Re-engineering the Help Desk	24.00	30.00	
The Computer Training Handbook	39.00	49.00	
The Inbound Telephone Call Center	35.95	35.95	
Support Automation Technology Report	265.00	295.00	
Managing Software Support	24.00	32.00	
High Performance Management	24.00	32.00	
We're Off to Seize the Wizard: The Revolution in Service Automation	90.00	99.00	
Help! The Art of Computer Technical Support	18.00	20.00	
The Help Desk Planner	175.00'	219.00	

Ordered By (Bill To)

Name:

_____

Title:

_____

Company:

_____

Address:

_____

(UPS does not ship to box
numbers, street no. req'd.)
City:

_____

State:_____ Zip:_____
Country: _____
Phone:_____
HDI Member Number:

_____

Ship To: (If different)

Name:

_____

Title:

_____

Company:

_____

Address:

_____

(UPS does not ship to box
numbers, street no. req'd.)
City:

_____

State: _____ Zip: _____
Country:_____
Phone:_____
HDI Member Number:

_____

PC Magazine Guide to Linking Lans	35.95	39.95		
PC Magazine Guide to Connectivity (Ed. II)	35.95	39.95		
PC Magazine Guide to Using Netware	35.95	39.95		
PC Magazine Guide to Using Windows 3.1	25.00	27.95		
PC Magazine Guide to Modem Communications	26.95	29.95		
HDI 12 0z. Mug (Blue with Platinum trim)	5.00	5.00		
HDI Embroidered Cap	10.00	10.00		
HDI Polo Shirt - Please order size and color	20.00	20.00		

❑ S ❑ M ❑ L ❑ XL ❑ XXL

❑ Lightt Blue ❑ Royal Blue ❑ Pink
❑ Jade ❑ Fuchsia ❑ Turquoise

Tax exempt organizations enter tax exempt here: _____

Sub-Total for all items	

Following US state residents please add state & local tax: CA, CO, CT, GA, IL, IN, KY, MA, MN, NC, NJ, NM, NY, OH, PA, TX, VA, WA, WI. Canadian residents please add 7% tax

SHIPPING & HANDLING (Allow 4-6 weeks for delivery)
$7.00 for UPS ground, waived on pre-paid orders. Call us for overnight or special shipping charges. Overseas shipping costs will vary by weight; we will add these costs to your order.

Total Payment

* First copy (or subscription) free with HDI membership

Help Desk Institute®

Training, educational materials and a networking forum for Help Desk professionals.

IT'S EASY TO ORDER

Quantity Discounts

10% discount when ordering 10 to 25 books of the same title. Need more than 25 of any one title? Please call for information about discounts.

Questions? Call:

From the US and Canada, call 800-248-5667. Worldwide, call 719-531-5138.

How to order:

Mail or FAX 719-528-4250 the completed order fom, indicating payment method to:

Help Desk Institute
1755 Telstar Drive
Suite 101
Colorado Springs, CO
80920-1017

Help Desk Institute Bookstore Order Form

ITEM	Member Price	Non-Member Price	Qty.	Cost
Help Desk U© 101 Kit Customer Service Skills for Help Desk Professionals	$995.00	$1095.00		
HDU 101 Additional Learner's Workbooks	39.95	49.95		
HDU 101 Additional videos	99.95	99.95		
Help Desk U© 102 Kit Successful Problem Solving Techniques for Help Desk Professionals	995.00	1095.00		
HDU 102 Additional Learner's Workbooks	39.95	49.95		
HDU 102 Additional videos	99.95	99.95		
Help Desk U© 201 Kit How to Manage and Improve Help Desk Operations	995.00	1095.00		
HDU 201 Additional Learner's Workbooks	39.95	49.95		
HDU 201 Additional videos	99.95	99.95		
HDI Video Seminar with Malcolm Fry: Set of 6 tapes	795.00	895.00		
The Help Desk Handbook	49.95	150.00		
LifeRaft Newsletter, one-year	36.00	96.00		
1993 Help Desk Buyers Guide	50.00	95.00		
1993 Help Desk Practices Survey	25.00	150.00		
1993 Help Desk Salary Survey	25.00	150.00		

More selections on following pages ...

METHOD OF PAYMENT

❑ Please Invoice
   my company
❑ Check enclosed
❑ Visa ❑ Mastercard
❑ American Express

Card # / P.O. #:

_____

Expiration Date:

_____

Signature:

_____

OUR GUARANTEE!

Should any book or gift item not meet your requirements, you will receive a full refund by returning it in reusable condition within 30 days of purchase.

HDI Focus Book: Customer Service Skills for Technical Support Professionals	6.95	9.95	
HDI Focus Book: Stress Management for Customer Support Professionals	6.95	9.95	
HDI Focus Book: Marketing the Help Desk to Senior Managers and Customers	6.95	9.95	
HDI Focus Book: Motivating and Managing Help Desk Professionals	6.95	9.95	
HDI Focus Book: How to Select and Use Outsource Services for your Hlep Desk	6.95	9.95	
HDI Focus Book: How to Measure Customer Satisfaction	6.95	9.95	
Tips on Evaluating and Re-engineering the Help Desk	24.00	30.00	
The Computer Training Handbook	39.00	49.00	
The Inbound Telephone Call Center	35.95	35.95	
Support Automation Technology Report	265.00	295.00	
Managing Software Support	24.00	32.00	
High Performance Management	24.00	32.00	
We're Off to Seize the Wizard: The Revolution in Service Automation	90.00	99.00	
Help! The Art of Computer Technical Support	18.00	20.00	
The Help Desk Planner	175.00'	219.00	

Ordered By (Bill To)

Name:

_____

Title:

_____

Company:

_____

Address:

_____

(UPS does not ship to box
numbers, street no. req'd.)
City:

_____

State:_____ Zip:_____
Country: _____
Phone:_____
HDI Member Number:

_____

Ship To: (If different)

Name:

_____

Title:

_____

Company:

_____

Address:

_____

(UPS does not ship to box
numbers, street no. req'd.)
City:

_____

State: _____ Zip: _____
Country:_____
Phone:_____
HDI Member Number:

_____

PC Magazine Guide to Linking Lans	35.95	39.95		
PC Magazine Guide to Connectivity (Ed. II)	35.95	39.95		
PC Magazine Guide to Using Netware	35.95	39.95		
PC Magazine Guide to Using Windows 3.1	25.00	27.95		
PC Magazine Guide to Modem Communications	26.95	29.95		
HDI 12 0z. Mug (Blue with Platinum trim)	5.00	5.00		
HDI Embroidered Cap	10.00	10.00		
HDI Polo Shirt - Please order size and color	20.00	20.00		

❑ S   ❑ M   ❑ L   ❑ XL   ❑ XXL

❑ Lightt Blue   ❑ Royal Blue   ❑ Pink
❑ Jade   ❑ Fuchsia   ❑ Turquoise

Tax exempt organizations enter tax exempt here: _____

Sub-Total for all items

Following US state residents please add state & local tax: CA, CO,
CT, GA, IL, IN, KY, MA, MN, NC, NJ, NM, NY, OH, PA, TX, VA,
WA, WI. Canadian residents please add 7% tax

SHIPPING & HANDLING (Allow 4-6 weeks for delivery)
$7.00 for UPS ground, waived on pre-paid orders. Call us for over-
night or special shipping charges. Overseas shipping costs will
vary by weight; we will add these costs to your order.

Total Payment

* First copy (or subscription) free with HDI membership

Help Desk Institute.

Training, educational materials and a networking forum for Help Desk professionals.

IT'S EASY TO ORDER

Quantity Discounts

10% discount when ordering 10 to 25 books of the same title. Need more than 25 of any one title? Please call for information about discounts.

Questions? Call:

From the US and Canada, call 800-248-5667. Worldwide, call 719-531-5138.

How to order:

Mail or FAX 719-528-4250 the completed order fom, indicating payment method to:
*Help Desk Institute
1755 Telstar Drive
Suite 101
Colorado Springs, CO
80920-1017*

Help Desk Institute Bookstore Order Form

ITEM	Member Price	Non-Member Price	Qty.	Cost
Help Desk U© 101 Kit Customer Service Skills for Help Desk Professionals	$995.00	$1095.00		
HDU 101 Additional Learner's Workbooks	39.95	49.95		
HDU 101 Additional videos	99.95	99.95		
Help Desk U© 102 Kit Successful Problem Solving Techniques for Help Desk Professionals	995.00	1095.00		
HDU 102 Additional Learner's Workbooks	39.95	49.95		
HDU 102 Additional videos	99.95	99.95		
Help Desk U© 201 Kit How to Manage and Improve Help Desk Operations	995.00	1095.00		
HDU 201 Additional Learner's Workbooks	39.95	49.95		
HDU 201 Additional videos	99.95	99.95		
HDI Video Seminar with Malcolm Fry: Set of 6 tapes	795.00	895.00		
The Help Desk Handbook	49.95	150.00		
LifeRaft Newsletter, one-year	36.00	96.00		
1993 Help Desk Buyers Guide	50.00	95.00		
1993 Help Desk Practices Survey	25.00	150.00		
1993 Help Desk Salary Survey	25.00	150.00		

More selections on following pages ...

METHOD OF PAYMENT

❑ **Please Invoice my company**
❑ **Check enclosed**
❑ **Visa** ❑ **Mastercard**
❑ **American Express**

Card # / P.O. #:

_____

Expiration Date:

_____

Signature:

_____

███████████████

OUR GUARANTEE!

Should any book or gift item not meet your requirements, you will receive a full refund by returning it in reusable condition within 30 days of purchase.

HDI Focus Book: Customer Service Skills for Technical Support Professionals	6.95	9.95	
HDI Focus Book: Stress Management for Customer Support Professionals	6.95	9.95	
HDI Focus Book: Marketing the Help Desk to Senior Managers and Customers	6.95	9.95	
HDI Focus Book: Motivating and Managing Help Desk Professionals	6.95	9.95	
HDI Focus Book: How to Select and Use Outsource Services for your Hlep Desk	6.95	9.95	
HDI Focus Book: How to Measure Customer Satisfaction	6.95	9.95	
Tips on Evaluating and Re-engineering the Help Desk	24.00	30.00	
The Computer Training Handbook	39.00	49.00	
The Inbound Telephone Call Center	35.95	35.95	
Support Automation Technology Report	265.00	295.00	
Managing Software Support	24.00	32.00	
High Performance Management	24.00	32.00	
We're Off to Seize the Wizard: The Revolution in Service Automation	90.00	99.00	
Help! The Art of Computer Technical Support	18.00	20.00	
The Help Desk Planner	175.00'	219.00	

Ordered By (Bill To)
Name:
_____

Title:
_____

Company:
_____

Address:
_____

(UPS does not ship to box
numbers, street no. req'd.)
City:

_____

State:_____ Zip:_____
Country: _____
Phone:_____
HDI Member Number:

_____

Ship To: (If different)
Name:
_____

Title:
_____

Company:
_____

Address:
_____

(UPS does not ship to box
numbers, street no. req'd.)
City:

_____

State: _____ Zip: _____
Country:_____
Phone:_____
HDI Member Number:

_____

Item				
PC Magazine Guide to Linking Lans	35.95	39.95		
PC Magazine Guide to Connectivity (Ed. II)	35.95	39.95		
PC Magazine Guide to Using Netware	35.95	39.95		
PC Magazine Guide to Using Windows 3.1	25.00	27.95		
PC Magazine Guide to Modem Communications	26.95	29.95		
HDI 12 0z. Mug (Blue with Platinum trim)	5.00	5.00		
HDI Embroidered Cap	10.00	10.00		
HDI Polo Shirt - Please order size and color	20.00	20.00		

❑ S ❑ M ❑ L ❑ XL ❑ XXL

❑ Lightt Blue ❑ Royal Blue ❑ Pink
❑ Jade ❑ Fuchsia ❑ Turquoise

Tax exempt organizations enter tax exempt here: _____

Sub-Total for all items

Following US state residents please add state & local tax: CA, CO, CT, GA, IL, IN, KY, MA, MN, NC, NJ, NM, NY, OH, PA, TX, VA, WA, WI. Canadian residents please add 7% tax

SHIPPING & HANDLING (Allow 4-6 weeks for delivery)
$7.00 for UPS ground, waived on pre-paid orders. Call us for over-night or special shipping charges. Overseas shipping costs will vary by weight; we will add these costs to your order.

Total Payment

* First copy (or subscription) free with HDI membership

The Help Desk Handbook

Evaluation

Ratings

	Poor	Fair	Average	Good	Very Good	Excellent
Organization and flow of content?	☐	☐	☐	☐	☐	☐
Quality of content?	☐	☐	☐	☐	☐	☐
Quality of illustrative materials?	☐	☐	☐	☐	☐	☐
Author's knowledge of subject?	☐	☐	☐	☐	☐	☐

Would you recommend this book to others? _____ If not, why not? _____

_____

What specific information was most beneficial to you?

_____

_____

What could have been done differently to make this book more worthwhile for you?

_____

_____

Please indicate your overall evaluation of this book.
(Circle One)

   Excellent   Good   Satisfactory   Unsatisfactory

Please use the space below to share other comments or reactions you have toward the *Help Desk Handbook*:

_____

_____

_____

May we use your name and comments for future marketing purposes? _____

Name: _____ Title: _____

Organization: _____ City and State/Province: _____

**Thank you for supporting Help Desk Institute by participating in this evaluation,
and for providing us with your valuable feedback!**

B U S I N E S S   R E P L Y   M A I L

FIRST CLASS MAIL   PERMIT NO. 3   COLORADO SPRINGS, CO

POSTAGE WILL BE PAID BY ADDRESSEE

Help Desk Institute

1755 Telstar Drive, Suite 101
Colorado Springs, CO 80920-9829